I0236601

First published in 2017 by Barrallier Books Pty Ltd,
trading as Echo Books

Registered Office: 35-37 Gordon Avenue, West Geelong, Victoria 3220, Australia.

www.echobooks.com.au

Copyright ©Marcus Fielding

Creator: Fielding, Marcus, author.

Title: Comrades in Arms and Rugby: The remarkable achievements of the 1919 Australian Imperial Force Rugby Union Squad/Marcus Fielding.

ISBN: 9780648308287 (hardcover)

A catalogue record for this book is available from the National Library of Australia

Book layout and design by Peter Gamble, Canberra.
Set in Garamond Premier Pro Display, 12/17 and Minerva Small Caps.

www.echobooks.com.au

COMRADES IN ARMS AND RUGBY

The remarkable achievements of the 1919 Australian Imperial Force
Rugby Union Squad

Marcus Fielding

ECHO BOOKS

Contents

Contents (cont)

Foreword

By Brigadier Ben James, AM, DSM
President of the Australian Army Rugby Union

For almost a century, Rugby Union has played a central role in developing the character and values we seek in our soldiers.

Today we define that character through values such as Courage, Initiative, Respect and Teamwork. We place great credence in the qualities that rugby imbues in our people—resilience, selflessness and comradeship.

When the Australian Imperial Force (AIF) was at the peak of its size and capability, Rugby provided an opportunity for soldiers to relax away from the trenches. While providing a welcome respite from duty, the game itself continued to reinforce the values and behaviours that even today we seek to inspire and develop in our people.

Our earlier book, *In the Field and On the Field* traced the evolution of Rugby Union in the Australian Army. In producing that publication, the story of the 1919 AIF Rugby Union squad became apparent—again. In 1919 the players in this squad were household names in Australia and it has been a privilege to rediscover the story of these remarkable soldiers and athletes.

Because this Rugby Union squad was selected from across the five AIF divisions in France, we have set this as the first time that a truly representative Australian Army Rugby Union Team was formed -and to that end we are pleased to celebrate our Centenary in 2019.

I am pleased to present this fascinating book, *Comrades in Arms and Rugby* as one marker of this tremendous milestone.

Foreword

By Lieutenant General Rick Burr, AO, DSC, MVO
Patron of the Australian Army Rugby Union

The Australian Army is central to the story of our nation and our people remain the core of our collective capability. Team sports such as rugby develop the qualities and values we seek in our men and women, and I am delighted to provide this foreword to *Comrades in Arms and Rugby*, the story of the men from the 1st Australian Imperial Force who came together to form Army's first representative rugby team in 1919.

Our profession demands the highest standards of excellence, a commitment to the team above self and an unwavering desire to reach our individual and collective potential. Rugby shines a light on these endeavours and many of Army's officers and soldiers, men and women have represented Australia at the highest levels, playing for the Wallabies and the Wallaroos. We can all be proud of their achievements.

It gives me tremendous pleasure that the story of the 1919 Australian Imperial Force Rugby Union Squad has been researched and produced in this impressive book. Their achievements are a fitting reminder of our organisation's evolving story, but equally demonstrate that the quality of our people remains the central feature of Army's capability.

Introduction

In early 1919 the call went out across the 160,000 strong Australian Imperial Force (AIF) based in Europe—'The war is over and it's time to get back into rugby.' The word went down the chain of command of five battle-hardened divisions—'We need your best. There's a different kind of battle to be fought before we go home.' Across France, Belgium and the United Kingdom AIF rugby teams played for the honour to represent their units, then their brigades, then their divisions and finally to represent the AIF.

This is the story of how the 1919 AIF Rugby Union Squad was formed, and how and where they played in France, the United Kingdom and in Australia. The teams were the first truly representative teams from across the Australian Army of the day. It is fitting that these teams were formed when the Australian Army was at the apogee of its size, experience and reputation.

The 1919 AIF Rugby Union Squad played a match against the French Army on 19 January 1919 and went on to play 28 matches across the United Kingdom before returning to Australia and playing an additional eight matches. Across these games the squad members established a reputation for hard but disciplined rugby. They inspired spectators and contributed directly to the re-invigoration of rugby union in the United Kingdom as well as Australia in the immediate post-war period.

Each man in the squad was as hard as the next. Most had endured four long years of war; many had been wounded. They played not only for their country but for the many mates they had lost during the war. Any sense of survivor's guilt was expressed in playing rugby as hard and fast as you possibly could.

The Australian Army Rugby Union (AARU) traces its origins to the 1919 AIF Rugby Union Squad. The AARU not only embodies the spirit of the 1919 AIF Teams, it continues to build on their tradition of wartime resilience, tenacity and team work.

Rugby Union after the Armistice on 11 November 1918

When the First World War ended on 11 November 1918 Allied military authorities were keen to ensure that the millions of soldiers awaiting repatriation and demobilisation across Europe were appropriately occupied and that the reputation of the force not be undermined by ill-disciplined behaviour. The challenge was particularly acute for Australian, New Zealand, Canadian, South African and Indian soldiers as shipping to take them home was scarce. Lietenant-General Sir John Monash had command of over 200,000 Australian troops in France , Belgium, England and the Middle East and the wait was unfortunately going to be longer than hoped.

The Australian Imperial Force (AIF) commanders quickly placed emphasis on encouraging all forms of healthy sport during the immediate post-Armistice period. A flurry of inter-platoon and inter-company competitions got underway. Up to then any games had been limited to within units while they were resting from serving in the front lines.

Early in 1919 the supreme British Command established the British Expeditionary Force Sports Board whose objectives were to:

- Improve the physical fitness and mental well-being of the troops in the British Expeditionary Force
- Encourage competition in all branches of sport in which men will compete for the honour of their unit
- Instil the true principle of sport—play for your side and not for yourself
- Produce teams to compete in the Inter-Force Tournament to be held in England.

In January 1919, the AIF established a Sports Control Board, responsible for organising sports including Rugby Union, Australian Rules Football, 'Association Football' (soccer), cross-country running, boxing, rowing, and rifle shooting competitions among others. Much of the organisation of these events occurred under the leadership of the 19th Battalion's Major Sydney Middleton who had a distinguished reputation in both rowing and rugby and was appointed the Organising Secretary. The Australian Comforts Fund provided the major portion of the costs for the competitions.

For units raised in NSW and Queensland, Rugby Union drew great support and inter-battalion and inter-brigade competitions were soon in full swing. At the same time the AIF was invited at short notice to play against a French Army team and the story of this team and match is the subject of a latter chapter.

In March, 1919, a formal Australian Corps Rugby Competition commenced in France. It comprised of one team from each five AIF divisions plus one from Corps Troops. The divisions and their units were scattered around the French countryside, but once the competition got under way, each team was concentrated at a central village, usually near their divisional headquarters.

Conditions did not deter the players:

> ... the grounds were not by any means ideal. One day a game would be played on a field covered in a couple of inches of snow. At another time the snow would give place to a similar depth of mud, and yet again the ground would be frozen hard...the teams often had to undertake journeys of between [20] and [30] kilometres—and even more—over bumpy roads, and return after the game. The Army wagon was not by any means a well-upholstered or well-sprung conveyance, and it had no central heating arrangements ...

When the journey to and fro was too great to be undertaken in a day, the visiting team was quartered and entertained by the host division and their supporters in true Aussie style.

Over the space of several weeks the team of the Second Division went through the competition undefeated, scoring 96 points to 3 against. Their line was crossed only once, by the First Division.

At the conclusion of this Australian Corps Rugby Competition, a squad of some 45 players were selected to go into training in Chatelet, Belgium, in order that a team might be selected to represent the Australian Corps.

The Fourth Army, to which the Australian Corps was attached, then invited the AIF to supply a team to represent the them in a match against the Second Army—a part of the post-war occupation force in Cologne, Germany.

Captain John Lane from the 18th Battalion was placed in command of the 31 men who were selected. They were billeted together for a short period of training and then defeated the Second Army XV by 21 points to 6. Sadly, no photographic record of this team or the match exists. Afterwards, the players enjoyed some leave in Cologne and played an additional match against the Royal Air Force units attached to the Second Army, winning 41 points to nil.

There is no record of an Australian Corps Rugby Team playing another Allied corps or team in the first half of 1919. Perhaps the parallel formation of two AIF Rugby Union Teams to tour through the United Kingdom between February and early May 1919 (the subject of a later chapter) was regarded as sufficient.

The Inter-Allied Games were held from 22 June to 6 July 1919 at the newly constructed Pershing Stadium just outside of Paris. The event was only open to participation by military personnel who were currently serving or had formerly served in the Allied Armies during the Great War. Australia was relatively advanced in its repatriation arrangements by this time and, as a consequence, only entered 63 contestants into track and field events, cross-country, swimming, tennis, boxing, wrestling, tug of war, rowing and hand-grenade throwing competitions. For reasons unknown, Australia did not compete in the shooting, water polo, horse riding, fencing, basketball, golf, baseball, soccer, or rugby union competitions.

The Match between the AIF 'Trench' Team and the French Army on 19 January 1919

Early in January 1919, the AIF received an invitation to play the French Army XV in Paris on the 19th. Time to select and prepare an Australian XV was short, so the five Australian divisions were asked to each nominate their eight best players—four forwards and four backs. The selectors were Colonel Thomas Blamey, Lieutenant Colonel Robert Massie and Major (Doctor) 'Wally' Matthews.

Matthews was chosen to manage the squad which concentrated at the School of Physical and Recreational Training at Barbencon near Charleroi, Belgium. Former Wallaby James 'Jimmy' Clarken and uncapped Wallaby Munro 'Munnie' Frazer were appointed coaches.

Massie was regarded as Australia's finest all-round athlete before the war and put the squad through a strenuous two weeks of training and trials. The squad played two matches against each other every day.

From this squad a team of 19 was selected and became known as the AIF Trench Team. The team members were:

- Company Sergeant Major Peter Buchanan—Halfback and Captain
- Lieutenant John Baird—Forward
- Quartermaster Sergeant John 'Plumb' Bond—Forward
- Gunner Henry Lenthall—Forward
- Lieutenant Ernest 'Bill' Cody—Forward
- Sergeant Godfrey 'Babe' See—Forward
- Lieutenant William 'Bill' O'Toole—Forward
- Lance Corporal John 'Bluey' Thompson—Forward
- Corporal Vivian 'Viv' Dunn—Forward
- Private Herbert 'Tom' Quinn—Forward
- Private Arthur 'Togo' Lyons—Forward
- Private Thomas 'Rat' Flannagan—Halfback
- Lieutenant Hunter Kirke—Halfback
- Corporal Joseph Stevenson—Three quarters
- Gunner James 'Jimmy' Bosward—Three quarters
- Private Peter 'Darky' Noels—Three quarters
- Corporal Dudley 'Dud' Suttor—Wing
- Driver Charles 'Nuggety' Leahey—Wing
- Captain Bruce 'Jackie' Beith—Fullback

The match against the French Army XV was a spectacle of hard, fast rugby—despite the chilly conditions. The score of 6–3 in favour of the AIF Trench Team hardly reflected their overall superiority. The Australians were consistently on the offensive during the match. It was only their lack of concerted action as a team that prevented them from capitalising more so on the opportunities they created. The short time they had spent training together was distinctly apparent. Credit on the other hand must be given to the determined defensive efforts of the French Army XV who repulsed numerous onslaughts against their line.

Sadly, no photographic record of the AIF Trench Team or this match exists.

The King's Cup for Rugby

At a meeting in the War Office in Whitehall in late January 1919, it was agreed that there were sufficient players of quality available to institute an Inter-Service and Dominion Forces Rugby Competition.

A subsequent meeting of the various arms of both the Services and Dominions was held at the Junior United Services Club on 8 February 1919, where Australia was represented by Major Wally Matthews, and final arrangements for the Competition made, dates and grounds allotted and fixtures drawn.

The Competition would include six teams: the New Zealand Army, the British Army (known during the competition as the Mother Country), the Australian Imperial Force, the Canadian Expeditionary Force, the South African Force and the Royal Air Force.

King George V agreed to lend his insignia and status to the Competition, as he did for all the other major sports. From that time the Inter-Service and Dominion Forces Rugby Competition was more commonly called the 'King's Cup for Rugby'.

Group portrait of the AIF Headquarters Team which opposed the Australian 'French' Team at Chiswick Ground on 12 February 1919.
Back row (left to right): Lieutenant Ryan; Sergeant Carpenter; Corporal Stewart; Corporal Gray; Private Watts; Corporal Gwynne.
Middle row: Corporal Tapp; Staff Sergeant Osborne; Sergeant Wheatley; Sergeant Murray; Gunner Jack Watkins;
Sergeant Frendin; Corporal Stenning.
Front row: Corporal Simpson; Private Noble; Private Locke. (AWM D00259)

Each team would play each other over a period of weeks in varying locations around Britain. Once the teams had played each encounter, the two sides with the most wins would face each other for the right to play for the King's Cup at Twickenham. The winner of the final would then play the French Army team at Twickenham.

A sub-committee was appointed to direct the Australian effort, consisting of Major Wally Matthews, Major Keith Norman and Lieutenant Leslie Seaborn, MC.

It now became necessary to select the best possible side to represent Australia. The AIF Headquarters Team in London had already played a number of matches against other Allied teams and done well, but

Group portrait of the AIF 'French' Team which opposed AIF Headquarters team at Chiswick Ground on 12 February 1919.

Back row (left to right): Gunner James 'Jimmy' Bosward; Lieutenant William 'Bill' Cody; Lance Corporal Vivian 'Viv' Dunn; Driver James 'Jimmy' Clarken; Sergeant William 'Roger' Bradley; Lieutenant William 'Bill' O'Toole: Lieutenant William 'Billy' Watson.

Middle row: Private Arthur 'Togo' Lyons; Sergeant Dudley 'Dud' Suttor; Private Charles 'Nuggetty' Leahey; Company Sergeant Major Peter Buchanan (Team Captain); Captain Bruce 'Jackie' Beith; Private Joseph Stephenson; Private John 'Bluey' Thompson.

Front row: Private Thomas 'Rat' Flannagan; Quartermaster Sergeant John 'Plumb' Bond. (AWM D00260)

there was also the AIF Trench Team which had beaten the French Army XV in Paris. Neither was regarded as an all-round first class combination, but both contained some excellent material.

So, on 28 January 1919, the AIF Trench Team travelled to England, where it met up with the AIF Headquarters Team. The combined squad was housed at Warwick Square, adjacent to the Westminster School, and trained on Chiswick Park.

On 12 February 1919 the two teams squared off in a match at Chiswick Park to assist selectors to compare talent. For this match the Trench Team renamed

Members of the AIF Team which defeated the South African Army Team by nine points to eight at Queen's Club, England on 19 February 1919. [Note the kangaroo emblem on the jerseys.]
Back row (left to right): Private Arthur 'Togo' Lyons; Corporal John 'Darb' Hickey; Corporal Vivian 'Viv' Dunn; Lieutenant Ernest 'Bill' Cody; Sergeant Joseph Murray; Lieutenant Martin.

Middle row: Private Peter 'Darky' Noels; Private Alma 'Ray' Elliott; Driver James 'Jimmy' Clarken; Lieutenant William 'Billy' Watson; Corporal Thomas 'Tom' Stenning; Lance Corporal John 'Bluey' Thompson.

Front row: Private Thomas 'Rat' Flannagan; Lieutenant Horace 'Dick' Pountney; Private Hayes. (AWM D00265)

Members of the AIF First XV competing in the King's Cup Competition taken in early March 1919.

Back row (left to right): Lance Corporal John 'Bluey' Thompson; Corporal Thomas 'Tom' Stenning; Lieutenant William 'Billy' Watson; Lieutenant Ernest 'Bill' Cody; Sergeant Joseph Murray; Lieutenant William 'Roger' Bradley; Corporal Arthur 'Togo' Lyons; Captain Bruce 'Jackie' Beith.

Middle row: Quartermaster Sergeant John 'Plumb' Bond; Corporal John 'Darb' Hickey; Company Sergeant Major Peter Buchanan; Gunner Jack Watkins; Sergeant Godfrey 'Babe' See.

Front row: Corporal Dudley 'Dud' Suttor; Private Thomas 'Rat' Flanagan. (AWM D00373)

themselves as the 'French' Team and won by twelve points to six.

After a series of trials two new AIF teams were formed: the AIF First XV and what became known as the AIF Reserve Team. Major Wally Matthews would manage the AIF First XV which would compete in the King's Cup for Rugby. Lieutenant Leslie Seaborn would manage the AIF Reserve Team which would tour the UK and Ireland. Some players moved between the two teams over the course of the next several weeks.

The draw for the King's Cup resulted in Australia being pitted against the Mother Country at Leicester on 8 March 1919, South Africa on 15 March at Newport, New Zealand on 22 March at Bradford, the Royal Air Force on 29 March at Gloucester, and Canada on 15 April at Twickenham.

Under the direction of Wally Matthews, the AIF First XV played the following train-up matches and developed a healthy spirit of camaraderie:

- The Australian Flying Corps at Gloucester, England on 15 February 1919. Win 50-nil.
- The South African Army Team at Queen's Club, England on 19 February 1919. Win 9-8.
- Leicester County at Leicester, England on 22 February 1919. Win 8-6.
- New Zealand Army A Team at Richmond, England on 26 February 1919. Loss 9-nil.

The King's Cup for Rugby commenced on 1 March 1919 with a match between New Zealand and the Royal Air Force, the former team winning

For the King's Cup Competition the AIF Squad was issued with a light blue jersey with the AIF 'Rising Sun' badge on the left breast.

Australia versus the Mother Country– 8 March 1919

For the match against the Mother Country at Leicester, England on 8 March 1919, the AIF First XV team members were:

- Lieutenant William 'Billy' Watson—Forward and Captain
- Quatermaster Sergeant John 'Plumb' Bond—Forward
- Private Arthur 'Togo' Lyons—Forward
- Lieutenant Ernest 'Bill' Cody—Forward
- Corporal Vivian 'Viv' Dunn—Forward
- Lance Corporal John 'Bluey' Thompson—Forward
- Sergeant Joseph Murray—Forward
- Sergeant Godfrey 'Babe' See—Forward
- Company Sergeant Major Peter Buchanan—Halfback
- Private Thomas 'Rat' Flannagan—Three quarters
- Corporal John 'Darb' Hickey—Three quarters
- Gunner Jack Watkins—Three quarters
- Corporal Dudley 'Dud' Suttor—Wing
- Corporal Thomas 'Tom' Stenning—Wing
- Captain Bruce 'Jackie' Beith—Fullback

The match was very evenly contested one, but the lack of combined effort on the part of the AIF players was apparent early in the game.

It was more noticeable in the case of the backs than with the forwards. The pack, in fact, worked exceedingly well and their keenness was at all times good to watch. They were lacking in finish and experience, however, and were badly served by their backs. The finish was most exciting, the Mother Country being awarded a penalty kick right under the AIF goal posts within a minute of the call of time. Scores were even up to that stage at three all. The kick was successful, and the Mother Country won by six points to three. Australia's score was an unconverted try by Thomas 'Tom' Stenning in the second half of the game. Nine thousand people watched the match which, as a first class exhibition of rugby, was disappointing

Australia versus South Africa— 15 March 1919

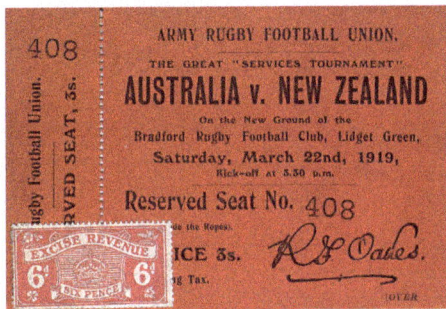

Ticket for the match between Australia and New Zealand scheduled for 22 March 1919.

The AIF made five changes for the next fixture against South Africa at Newport, England, on 15 March 1919. Sergeant William 'Roger' Bradley and Private Herbert 'Tom' Quinn took the places of Lance Corporal John 'Bluey' Thompson and Sergeant Joseph Murray in the forwards; the playing coach Major 'Wally' Matthews himself worked the scrum in place of Company Sergeant Major Peter Buchanan; and Lieutenant Horace 'Dick' Pountney and Gunner James 'Jimmy' Bosward came in at three quarters.

The Australians won a hard, clean game by eight points to five—a decided improvement on the match against the Mother Country. Although usually beaten in the scrum by the larger South African pack, the AIF forwards performed splendidly everywhere else, and it was mainly by their work that the game was won. The backs still lacked finish. Their passing was faulty and badly timed, and the finesse necessary to win big matches was not shown. Corporal Dudley 'Dud' Suttor and Lieutenant William 'Roger' Bradley were the try scorers for Australia, with Corporal Thomas 'Tom' Stenning converting Suttor's try.

According to the King's Cup draw, the next match was to be against New Zealand at Bradford, England, on 22 March 1919, but three inches of snow fell that day and the match was postponed until 9 April.

Practice match for the AIF Squad at Chiswick on 26 March 1919.

Identified (left to right): 1. Lieutenant John 'Jack' Ahearne; 2. Sergeant 'Pat' Egan; 3. Major Walter 'Wally' Mathews (umpire); 4. Lieutenant John Baird; 5. Driver James 'Jimmy' Clarken; 6. Captain Bruce 'Jackie' Beith (foreground); 7. Gunner Stewart; 8. Lieutenant William 'Bill' Cody; 9. Lieutenant William 'Billy' Watson (stripes); 10. Lieutenant William 'Bill' O'Toole (light shirt); 11. Lieutenant Irving Ormiston; 12. Corporal Vivian 'Viv' Dunn; 13. Sergeant McKerrigan; 14. Lance Corporal John 'Bluey' Thompson (stripes); 15. unidentified. (AWM D00521K)

Practice match for the AIF Squad at Chiswick on 26 March 1919.

Identified (left to right): 1. Corporal John. Robertson; 2. Lieutenant Horace 'Dick' Poutney (stripes); 3. Sergeant 'Pat' Egan; 4. Gunner James 'Jimmy' Bosward (stripes); 5. Lieutenant Irving Ormiston (carrying the ball); 6. Lieutenant William 'Billy' Watson; 7. Corporal Vivian 'Viv' Dunn; 8. Lieutenant William 'Bill' O'Toole (obscured by Dunn); 9. Sergeant William 'Roger' Bradley; 10. unidentified (stripes); 11. Private Arthur 'Togo' Lyons (light colour); 12. Quartermaster Sergeant John 'Plumb' Bond (stripes); 13. unidentified (beside Cody); 14. Lieutenant Ernest 'Bill' Cody; 15. Private Baskerville (stripes); 16. Driver James 'Jimmy' Clarken; 17. Lance Corporal John 'Bluey' Thompson (foreground); 18. Lieutenant John Baird. (AWM D00523K)

Practice match for the AIF Squad at Chiswick on 26 March 1919.

Identified (left to right): 1. Lance Corporal John 'Bluey' Thompson; 2. unidentified; 3. Gunner Stewart; 4. Sergeant 'Pat' Egan; 5. Lieutenant Horace 'Dick' Pountney (stripes); 6. Gunner James 'Jimmy' Bosward (stripes); 7. Captain Bruce 'Jackie' Beith (tackling); 8. Sergeant Dudley 'Dud' Suttor (striped jersey); 9. Corporal Joseph Stevenson (white jersey). (AWMD00524K)

Practice match for the AIF Squad at Chiswick on 26 March 1919.

Identified (left to right): 1. Private Baskerville, behind; 2. Gunner Stewart; 3. unidentified; 4. Lieutenant William 'Bill' O'Toole; 5. Quartermaster Sergeant John 'Plumb' Bond, striped jersey; 6. Private Arthur 'Togo' Lyons, white jersey; 7. Lieutenant Willian 'Billy' Watson; 8. Sergeant William 'Roger' Bradley; 9. Lieutenant Ernest 'Bill' Cody; 10. Corporal Vivian 'Viv' Dunn; 11. unidentified; 12. Sergeant Joseph Murray; 13. Lieutenant Stanley 'Stan' Ryan; 14. Sergeant McKerrigan; 15. Corporal John Robertson. (AWM D00525K)

Practice match for the AIF Squad at Chiswick on 26 March 1919.

Identified (left to right): 1. Major Walter 'Wally' Matthews, referee; 2. Driver James 'Jimmy' Clarken; 3. Lieutenant John Baird; 4. Sergeant Joseph Murray; 5. Corporal Vivian 'Viv' Dunn; 6. Private Baskerville; 7. Lieutenant William 'Billy' Watson; 8. Lieutenant Ernest 'Bill' Cody; 9. Lieutenant William 'Bill' O'Toole; 10. unidentified, obscured; 11. Sergeant William 'Roger' Bradley; 12. Lance Corporal John 'Bluey' Thompson; 13. Lieutenant Horace 'Dick' Pountney; 14. Lieutenant Stanley 'Stan' Ryan; 15. Private Arthur 'Togo' Lyons; 16. Sergeant Stephen 'Pat' Egan. (AWM D00526K)

Australia versus the Royal Air Force— 29 March 1919

The next game was against the Royal Air Force at Gloucester, England, on 29 March 1919. Changes for this match were Sergeant Stephen 'Pat' Egan for Corporal Thomas 'Tom' Stenning, who was injured, and Lance Corporal John 'Bluey' Thompson back in place of Private Herbert 'Tom' Quinn.

The Royal Air Force secured a surprise win scoring seven points (a field goal and penalty) to Australia's three (a try). The Australians certainly had a bad day, literally throwing away chance after chance of scoring through faulty work by the backs. Again the pack was superior to the opposition, both in the loose and in the ruck, but there was absolutely no cohesion between the forwards and the backs. Corporal Dudley 'Dud' Suttor was the chief agent in a score by Lieutenant William 'Billy' Watson, passing the ball to him at the right time after a good run. The Royal Air Force did not cross the Australians' line.

Members of the AIF First XV competing in the King's Cup Competition taken in early April 1919.

Back row (left to right): Driver James 'Jimmy' Clarken; Gunner James 'Jimmy' Bosward; Lieutenant William 'Roger' Bradley; Sergeant Joseph Murray; Corporal Vivian 'Viv' Dunn; Lieutenant Ernest 'Bill' Cody; Corporal Arthur 'Togo' Lyons; Sergeant Godfrey 'Babe' See.

Middle row: Corporal Thomas 'Tom' Stenning; unidentified; Major (Doctor) Walter 'Wally' Matthews (in uniform); Lieutenant William 'Billy' Watson; Captain Bruce 'Jackie' Beith; unidentified; Corporal Dudley 'Dud' Suttor; unidentified (in uniform).

Front row: Private Thomas 'Rat' Flannagan; Quartermaster Sergeant John 'Plumb' Bond; Lieutenant Horace 'Dick' Pountney; unidentified child; Lieutenant Daniel 'Dan' Carroll, unidentified.

Insert: Lance Corporal John 'Bluey' Thompson. (Soldiers and Sportsmen)

Australia versus Canada – 5 April 1919

To take on the Canadians at Twickenham, England, on 5 April 1919, the AIF Firs XV team members were:

- Lieutenant William 'Billy' Watson—Forward and Captain
- Sergeant William 'Roger' Bradley—Forward
- Lance Corporal John 'Bluey' Thompson—Forward
- Lieutenant Ernest 'Bill' Cody—Forward
- Private Arthur 'Togo' Lyons—Forward
- Corporal Vivian 'Viv' Dunn—Forward
- Quartermaster Sergeant John 'Plumb' Bond—Forward
- Sergeant Godfrey 'Babe' See—Forward
- Private Thomas 'Rat' Flannagan—Halfback
- Corporal John Robertson—Five Eight
- Lieutenant Horace 'Dick' Pountney—Three quarters
- Sergeant Stephen 'Pat' Egan—Three quarters
- Lieutenant Daniel 'Dan' Carroll—Wing
- Corporal Dudley 'Dud' Suttor—Wing
- Captain Bruce 'Jackie' Beith—Fullback

The Prince of Wales and Prince Albert watched this match. The highlight of which was the first appearance of Lieutenant Daniel 'Dan' Carroll, the winner of two Olympic Gold Medals for rugby and who had been seconded from the U.S. Army.

The Canadians were hopelessly outclassed, to the extent of thirty-eight points to nil. It was the first time that the Australians 'clicked' as a team and played the first class rugby of which they were capable. The forwards and backs worked with a perfect understanding and had their opponents on the defensive throughout the whole game. Tries in this match were scored by Corporal Dudley 'Dud' Suttor (2), Corporal John Robertson (2), Sergeant William 'Roger' Bradley (2), Corporal Vivian 'Viv' Dunn,

Quartermaster Sergeant John 'Plumb' Bond, Sergeant Stephen 'Pat' Egan and Lieutenant Daniel 'Dan' Carroll. Lance Corporal John 'Bluey' Thompson converted three of these tries and Sergeant William 'Roger' Bradley one.

After the match the two Princes came onto the field and spent some time in conversation with all the players. The Prince of Wales was a very popular man with the Diggers.

Prince Edward VIII (Prince of Wales) accompanied by Prince Albert (Duke of York) meeting Team Captain William 'Billy' Watson (centre) and Bruce 'Jackie' Beith (far right) at Twickenham, England, on 5 April 1919.

Australia versus New Zealand— 9 April 1919

Up to this stage of the King's Cup competition, New Zealand had won all four matches they had played, while the Mother Country had won three and had a good chance of beating South Africa. It only remained for the New Zealanders to beat the Australians in their match at Bradford, England, and the King's Cup would have been their property without having to play any more matches. The newspapers in the UK were almost unanimous in their opinions that New Zealand had the ability to win comfortably. However, the fast improving Australians were destined to be the fly in the New Zealand ointment. The AIF First XV Team members were:

- Lieutenant William 'Billy' Watson—Forward and Captain
- Sergeant William 'Roger' Bradley—Forward
- Lance Corporal John 'Bluey' Thompson—Forward
- Lieutenant Ernest 'Bill' Cody—Forward
- Driver James 'Jimmy' Clarken—Forward
- Corporal Vivian 'Viv' Dunn—Forward
- Sergeant Joseph Murray—Forward
- Sergeant Godfrey 'Babe' See—Forward

New Zealand attacking in the match between Australia and New Zealand at Bradford, England, on 9 April 1919. Note the sizeable crowd.
Identified (left to right): Lieutenant Daniel 'Dan' Carroll (crouching right); Sergeant Stephen 'Pat' Egan (running left);Lieutenant Horace 'Dick' Pountney (running left); Private A. Singe, New Zealand (NZ), passing the ball; Private Thomas 'Rat' Flannagan (running left); unidentified, partly obscured; Leonard 'Jack' Stohr, NZ (running left). (AWM D00534)

New Zealand chasing a grub kick in the match between Australia and New Zealand at Bradford, England, on 9 April 1919. (AWM D00537)

- Private Thomas 'Rat' Flannagan—Halfback
- Corporal John Robertson—Five Eighth
- Lieutenant Horace 'Dick' Pountney—Three quarters
- Sergeant Stephen 'Pat' Egan—Three quarters
- Lieutenant Daniel 'Dan' Carroll—Wing
- Corporal Dudley 'Dud' Suttor—Wing
- Captain Bruce 'Jackie' Beith—Fullback

The match played on 9 April 1919 before 7000 people was the finest game of the King's Cup Competition. The final score was six points to five in favour of the Australians—the winners pressing hard at the final whistle.

The win may be attributed to Driver James 'Jimmy' Clarken who played only in this match of the King's Cup.

Line out in the match between Australia and New Zealand at Bradford, England, on 9 April 1919.
Identified (left to right): 1. Referee Mr Yeadon; 2. Ford, New Zealand (NZ); 3. Private Thomas 'Rat' Flannagan; 4. James 'Jimmy' Ryan, NZ; 5. Lance Corporal John 'Bluey' Thompson; 6. Private A. Singe, NZ (6); 7. Sergeant Godfrey 'Babe' See; 8. Lieutenant William 'Billy' Watson; 9. unidentified NZ forward; 10. Sergeant William 'Roger' Bradley; 11. Corporal Vivian 'Viv' Dunn; 12. Ernest Bellis, NZ; 13. Lieutenant Daniel 'Dan' Carroll; 14. Sergeant Joseph Murray; 15. unidentified NZ forward; 16. Driver James 'Jimmy' Clarken; 17. unidentified NZ forward. (AWM D00533K)

Winston McCarthy wrote this about the match:

> A story is told about the defeat by Australia. Among the Australian servicemen was Jimmy Clarken, NSW forward, who had played in New Zealand in 1905 with the touring Australian team, against New Zealand teams in Australia in 1905 and 1910 and against New Zealand Maoris in 1910. It will be appreciated that by 1919 Jimmy would be 43 years of age and getting to be long in the tooth for Rugby, but the Australians had the greatest respect for this tough little front ranker. They kept him in cotton wool and paraded him only when the going was tough. He insisted that he play in the King's Cup match against New Zealand. "Play me against them," he said, "and I'll guarantee I'll upset them so much in the front row and they'll get so little ball that they'll be snarling at each other."

> 'It must be realised', says McCarthy, 'that New Zealand then only packed two men in the front row against the opponents three. In the match, Clarken went in as hooker and at each scrum made sure that his head was in between the two New Zealanders opposite. That meant that at each scrum, Australia had the loose head whichever side the ball was put in. Starved of the ball, the New Zealand backs only scored one try.'

But there was more to it than just Jimmy Clarken's skill. There were six All Blacks in the New Zealand team. These included James 'Jimmy' Ryan and Charles Brown, both former All Black captains. The most capped was 'Ranji' Wilson described as the best loose forward pre-war in New Zealand; his ten caps were two against the Anglo-Welsh team and the rest against Australia.

Australia missing a conversion in the match between Australia and New Zealand at Bradford, England, on 9 April 1919. Identified (left to right): 1. Lieutenant Horace 'Dick' Pountney; 2. Lieutenant Ernest 'Bill' Cody; 3. Sergeant Godfrey 'Babe' See; 4. Private Thomas 'Rat' Flannagan; 5. Lieutenant Daniel 'Dan' Carroll; 6. Captain Bruce 'Jackie' Beith; 7. Lieutenant William 'Billy' Watson; Driver James 'Jimmy' Clarken; 9, 10, 11, 12, 13, 14 unidentified New Zealand players; 15. Corporal Vivian 'Viv' Dunn; 16. Sergeant William 'Roger' Bradley. (AWM D00536K)

The Australian forwards outplayed the Kiwi pack in every facet of the game and the backs showed their best form, with straight, strong running. In the first half of play, Lance Corporal John 'Bluey' Thompson and Sergeant Stephen 'Pat' Egan scored tries for Australia, neither of which was converted and the AIF Team led by this margin at the half-time interval.

Early in the second half, New Zealand's Percival Storey scored a fine try, converted by Leonard 'Jack' Stohr. From this point however, the Australians rallied and the game reached a point of high excitement. On many occasions the Australian forwards took play dangerously close to the New Zealand line with some mighty rushes and there was some spectacular passing rivalled only by the stubborn defence of the New Zealanders. There were no further additions to the score. New Zealand's loss placed them in the position of having to play another match if the Mother Country beat South Africa, which they did on 12 April 1919.

This match was the end of the King's Cup Competition as far as the Australians were concerned. It was generally conceded that they had been unfortunate in not having struck their form earlier in the competition. They defeated all the other Dominion teams in the contest by 52 points to 10 against; but the loss to the Royal Air Force was inexplicable.

New Zealand played off with the Mother Country at Twickenham, England, on 16 April 1919 and won the

Fullback Captain Bruce 'Jackie' Beith is tackled in the match between Australia and New Zealand and at Bradford, England, on 9 April 1919. Identified: 1. A. Wilson, New Zealand (NZ); 2. Referee Mr Yeadon; 3. Private A. Singe, NZ forward; 4. Captain Bruce 'Jackie' Beith; 5. unidentified NZ forward; 6. Sergeant Joseph Murray; 7. Corporal Vivian 'Viv' Dunn; 8. R. Sellars, NZ; 9. unidentified NZ, obscured; 10. Lieutenant Horace 'Dick' Pountney; 11. Lieutenant Ernest 'Bill' Cody; 12. Ernest Belliss, NZ. (AWM D00535)

game and the King's Cup by nine points to three. The King's Cup Competition of 15 matches was an immensely successful tournament, played in great spirits throughout. The Competition re-invigorated the popularity of rugby union in post-war England.

The King's Cup Competition was the first international rugby event involving several representative teams from the northern and southern hemispheres. It sowed the seed for a future Rugby World Cup; although, it took over 60 years for that seed to germinate, when the International Rugby Board finally approved an international rugby tournament in the mid-1980s.

Winning the King's Cup for Rugby gave New Zealand the right to represent the Armies of the

King George V presenting the King's Cup to James 'Jimmy' Ryan the captain of the New Zealand Services Rugby Team at Twickenham, England, on 16 April 1919.

The 1919 King's Cup for Rugby

King George V meets the French Army XV before their match
against New Zealand at Twickenham, England,
on 19 April 1919.

British Empire in a match against the French Army XV three days later at Twickenham on 19 April 1919, which the King attended—the New Zealanders winning 20-3.

After the King's Cup matches the AIF First XV continued to tour the UK and played the following matches:

- Devon County on 12 April 1919 at Exeter, England. Win 11-3.
- Royal Naval Depot on 16 April 1919 at Plymouth, England. Win 14-10.
- Maesteg on 19 April 1919 at Maesteg, Wales. Loss 18-3.
- Pill Harriers on 21 April 1919 at Newport, England. Loss 12-3.
- Abertillery on 23 April 1919 at Abertillery, Wales. Win 11-3.
- Ogmore Vale on 26 April 1919 at Ogmore Vale, Wales. Loss 6-3.
- Cornwall on 3 May 1919 at Penzance, England. Win 9-nil.

The AIF Reserve Team

As mentioned above, the AIF Reserve Team provided some players to the AIF First XV during the King's Cup Competition, but they also toured the United Kingdom in their own right between February and May 1919. Lieutenant Leslie Seaborn led and managed the AIF Reserve Team with great energy and Company Sergeant Major Peter Buchanan, after playing in the first King's Cup match against the Mother Country, then captained the AIF Reserve Team.

The AIF Reserve Team also established a fine reputation as a rugby force to be reckoned with. The success of the Reserve Team was impressive. The team played the following matches:

- AIF Depot, 15 February 1919 at Warminster. Win 19-10.
- 18th Wing Royal Air Force, 19 February 1919 at Hounslow. Win 52-nil.
- AIF Depots, 22 February 1919 at Warminster. Win 8-3.
- New Zealand Army B Team, 26 February 1919 at Richmond. Loss 17-3.
- Guy's Hospital, 8 March 1919 at Chiswick. Win 25-nil.
- Llanelly, 15 March 1919 at Llanelly. Win 11-nil.
- East Midlands, 29 March 1919 at Northampton. Win 27-11.
- Llanelly, 12 April 1919 at Llanelly. Loss 11-8.
- Exmouth, 19 April 1919 at Exeter. Win 21-3.

The AIF Reserve Team in early 1919.

Back row (left to right): unidentified; unidentified; Driver James 'Jimmy' Clarken (in uniform); unidentified; Gunner James 'Jimmy' Bosward; Lieutenant William 'Roger' Bradley; Sergeant Joseph Murray; Corporal Vivian 'Viv' Dunn; Lieutenant Ernest 'Bill' Cody; Corporal Arthur 'Togo' Lyons; Sergeant Godfrey 'Babe' See.

Middle row: Major (Doctor) Walter 'Wally' Matthews (in uniform); unidentified; unidentified; Lieutenant Irving 'Irv' Ormiston, Sergeant Joseph Murray; unidentified; unidentified; unidentified; unidentified; Lieutenant Leslie Seaborn (in uniform).

Front row: unidentified; unidentified; Company Sergeant Major Peter Buchanan; unidentified; Corporal Joseph Stevenson.

On ground: unidentified; unidentified; unidentified; unidentified.

(Soldiers and Sportsmen)

- Devon County, 21 April 1919 at Newton Abbott. Win 21-3.
- Teignmouth, 23 April 1919 at Teignmouth. Win 40-3.
- Llanelly, 3 May 1919 at Llanelly. Loss 17-3.

Of all their victories the most remarkable was their win over Llanelly at Llanelly's home ground on 15 March 1919—the first time this had ever been done by a touring team. Llanelly took their revenge in two subsequent matches on 12 April and 13 May 1919, but the AIF Reserve Team's great win must go down as an historic moment in Australia's rugby annals.

So concluded a wonderful period for the 1919 AIF Rugby Union squad. Over 40 players had had the opportunity to play at an international level and in doing so contributed to re-energising the popularity of rugby union in the UK. Their exploits had been followed avidly in the Australian press and pressure soon mounted for them to tour the major Australian rugby centres when they returned home.

The AIF Rugby Union Squad's Tour of Australia

In Australia as a result of the large number of rugby union players enlisting for the war, there was insufficient playing numbers to continue running a number of the district rugby competitions. A decision was made in late February 1915, with the following announcement being made from the New South Wales Rugby Union (NSWRU).

> At a special General Meeting held on Monday 1 March 1915, the NSWRU unanimously decided to suspend competition and play only a limited number of matches for the purpose of maintaining physical fitness among the members, and to devote one night per week in each district for drilling and military training and also to hold a number of Saturday afternoon parades on a central ground, in which all district squads would participate.

The Union's stance was uncompromising and based on the assumption that the continuation of sport would hinder enlistment. The announcement meant the only rugby union games that could be played were social, non-competitive matches, or junior matches. This policy was soon adopted by the Victorian Rugby Union (VRU) and a year later by Queensland Rugby Union (QRU).

This position differed from the New South Wales Rugby League, who announced that they would continue to provide 'sorely needed entertainment for a troubled public'. This decision was initially met with intense criticism.

However, the defeat of the Conscription Referenda in October 1916, and again in 1917, highlighted that the war did not have the support of the majority of the population, and this, coupled with the amateurism debate and the association of rugby union with the privileged middle class, confirmed to many the view that the NSWRU was out of touch with the average working person and had little concern for their welfare.

The NSWRU and QRU actively encouraged their players to 'join up' for patriotic reasons—the players responded in their thousands. The outcome was that, as the war progressed, the future of the game of rugby union was undermined by the loss of many fine young men at both club and representative level. Ten Wallabies, 17 NSW Waratahs, three Queensland Reds, as well as dozens of club level players were killed, together with the President of the NSWRU, Major Jim MacManamey. The famous old Glebe Club in Sydney, for example, was never able to resurface—of 67 Glebe players who enlisted, 27 were killed and 26 severely wounded, never to play again. It was estimated that around 5000 rugby players had joined the AIF and of these more than 500 had been killed.

Rugby league, meanwhile, became enormously popular, and was able to secure ground leases, develop new talent and build profits on which to develop the game. As rugby league continued to grow throughout the war many players and clubs, devastated by losses at Gallipoli and France, switched codes. In early 1918, the Central Queensland Rugby Union went over to rugby league.

In many rural areas, rugby league had become very well established. With many small towns suffering devastating losses due to the war there was little heart to restart the rugby union games. In some towns, such as Gunnedah, there would be a lapse of 30 years before a rugby union club was formed again.

By late 1918 rugby union in Australia was in a desperate state. Clubs were without many experienced officials and funds, players had not yet returned from overseas, and grounds were in tight supply. The NSWRU was even prohibited from meeting due to emergency measures caused by the influenza epidemic sweeping the world.

For the 1919 season, the NSWRU decided to suspend the strict pre-war district domiciliary regulations, hoping that this would give clubs some scope to re-form. The outcome was that six clubs did re-start to enter the First Grade competition (Eastern Suburbs, Glebe-Balmain, Manly, Sydney University, Cambridge and YMCA), four teams in the Second Grade and six junior competitions with 62 teams. A very frail start indeed with little or no income in sight. In Queensland an even tougher struggle to survive was taking place, many matches only fielding 13 or 14 men per team.

Into this depressing scenario then came the stunning news headlines of the magnificent performances of the AIF Rugby Union Squad in Europe. First was the victory over the French Army XV in Paris on 19 January 1919, the defeat of Llanelly at Llanelly on 15 March 1919, and then the defeat of New Zealand in the King's Cup Competition on 9 April 1919. Rugby union spirits in Australia were suddenly lifted; here in the AIF Squad we had a ready-made, champion national team, including, as it turned out, some great stars for the future.

Such was public demand to see the AIF Squad that the NSWRU and QRU made arrangements with a delighted Australian High Command to bring them back to Australia to play a series of exhibition matches in the main centres of each state. The triumphant tour that followed was special because it would not have happened if rugby union had not answered the call and if so many rugby players had not volunteered to enlist.

The AIF Squad left England in May 1919 and on the trip home their troopship called into Port Elizabeth, South Africa. There they played against the top South African province, Natal, at Durban, winning 34-3. The Australians appreciated the firm South African ground and ran in some spectacular tries.

Arriving in Sydney to great public acclaim in early July 1919, the team manager Major Walter 'Wally' Matthews, team captain Lieutenant William 'Billy' Watson and 35 members of what was by now a well-known and popular military and sporting entity were welcomed by a large gathering of rugby enthusiasts that included the secretary of the NSWRU.

The next day the AIF Squad enjoyed more accolades at an official government welcome held at the Australia Hotel and later that night enjoyed a night out at the theatre, having been invited to attend the J.C. Williamson production of *Goody two shoes*.

On Saturday 5 July 1919, before a crowd of 10 000, the AIF First XV played a representative NSW team. The NSWRU arranged for school children and returned soldiers 'with badges' to be admitted free to the game and made special arrangements for 'wounded men from the military hospitals.' The main match was preceded by a game between the AIF Reserve Team and a NSW Second XV, which NSW won 25-11.

In the main match NSW was soundly defeated by the AIF First XV 42-14. The *Sydney Morning Herald* reported on the outstanding record achieved by the AIF teams in Britain and France, stating that '...the Diggers thoroughly deserved the high reputation that had preceded them'...'the fifteen stands out as one of the greatest seen on Sydney grounds'.

The following Saturday 12 July 1919, at the University Oval, the AIF First XV played an Australian team

THE A.I.F RUGBY UNION FOOTBALL TEAM OF 1919

Back Row: Corp. Stenning (NSW), Sergt. G. Horsey(NSW) Sergt. W. Bradley (NSW), Corporal Dunn
(NSW), Lieutenant W. O'Toole (NSW), Lieutenant E.A. Cody (NSW), and T. Bosward (the referee).
Second Row: Gunner Rankin (Vic), C.S.M. P. Buchanan (NSW) Lieutenant W.T. Watson M.C. and Bar
and D.C.M. (NSW., capt.) Major W.F. Matthews (NSW Manager), Sergt. S. Egan (Qld), Lance-Corporal
J. Thompson (Qld), Gunner J.H. Bosward (NSW). Front Row: Lieutenant Pountney (NSW), Private J.
Flanagan (Qld), Sergt G. See (NSW), Sergt. D. Suttor (NSW) and Q.M.S. Bond (NSW). The only team to
defeat New Zealand, the winners of the Inter-Services Competition for the King's Cup.

Members of the AIF First XV during the Australian Tour (photo taken in early July 1919).

(The Referee)

chosen from NSW and Queensland, defeating it 28-18. The next day they visited the 'garden suburb for soldiers at Matraville' where they laboured for most of the day on various improvement projects:

> Stiff and sore from their exertions on the previous afternoon members of the AIF Rugby Union Team were early visitors to the garden suburb for soldiers at Matraville yesterday. Arming themselves with long handled shovels they spent a strenuous morning, and after being refreshed by luncheon returned to the attack in the afternoon. It had been expected that the team which represented Australia on Saturday against the Diggers would co-operate with the latter in assaulting a sand hill, but their absence was explained by more or less general exhaustion.

On 16 July 1919 the AIF First XV played a New England side in Armidale defeating it 35-11, before travelling to Brisbane where they defeated Queensland 38-7 on 19 July 1919 in front of a crowd of around 5000 spectators.

On 23 July 1919 the AIF First XV played a Queensland AIF Team (which included some of their own AIF Reserve Team) on the Brisbane Cricket Ground and defeated them 30-3. On 26 July 1919 they played again against Australia at the Brisbane Cricket Ground and defeated the joint Queensland-NSW team 20-13. On their way back to Sydney they played the North Western Association side on 30 July 1919 at the Showground in Inverell, defeating it 52-6. They completed their tour by defeating Australia once again by 22-6 on 2 August 1919 at the Sydney Sports Ground.

The AIF First XV won all eight of their matches— scoring 268 points with 78 scored against them. In the three games against Australia they scored 70 against 37. The top scorer for the AIF Team was Peter Buchanan, with 43 points, followed by John 'Plumb' Bond and Thomas 'Tom' Stenning, each with 30 points. As for the work-horses, John 'Plumb' Bond and Thomas 'Tom' Stenning played in all eight matches. Those playing all but one match included James 'Jimmy' Bosward, William 'Roger' Bradley, Peter Buchanan, Vivian 'Viv' Dunn, Horace 'Dick' Pountney, Clifford 'Cliff' Rankin and John 'Bluey' Thompson.

In every sense, the AIF First XV's tour of Australia was a resounding success and morale booster for rugby union. It was remarkable that the AIF veterans still had the capacity for tough and vigorous play after the basic diet, privation, stress and difficulties faced by them during years of active service. It was their last 'hurrah' as 'comrades in arms and in rugby' and when they separated to return to their homes—their war, finally, over.

But would rugby union in post-war Australia be able to recover from the significant loss of players and the momentum of the professional game of rugby league?

The majority of the AIF Squad members were from NSW and many of them returned to club rugby ranks. Queensland, by comparison, did not enjoy anywhere near this numerical injection and after some efforts during the 1919 season the QRU was forced to disband. It did not re-surface until the 1929 season.

Sir Henry Braddon, KBE, William Hill and James McMahon of the NSWRU, realised that rugby union in Australia could be best re-invigorated by NSW remaining on the world stage. The NSWRU organised incoming and outgoing international tours each year to keep the game alive. Exploiting the international fame of the AIF Squad, invitations were extended to both the New Zealand Rugby Football Union and the South African Rugby Football Union to tour in 1920 and 1921 respectively.

William 'Billy' Watson joined the Glebe-Balmain club and was appointed NSW Captain in 1920. Others from the AIF Team also went on to play for NSW including Peter Buchanan, Ernest 'Bill' Cody, Vivian 'Viv' Dunn, Bruce 'Jackie' Beith, Alma 'Ray' Elliott, Johnny 'Plumb' Bond and Dudley 'Dud' Suttor.

The first All Black team to visit Australia in 1920 proved to be one of the most brilliant New Zealand teams for a decade and included seven members of the Army side beaten by the AIF First XV during the 1919 King's Cup Competition. They won all seven matches in which they played, including one against NSW Country in Taree. They were just the tonic needed to regenerate interest in rugby union in Australia.

The 1921 season was equally interesting with the Springboks providing headlines. Their forwards were a huge lot and backs outstandingly fast. They regularly drew crowds of 20 000 to their matches.

That year, it became NSW's turn to tour New Zealand. This team turned in a remarkable result, losing only one of their 10 tour matches and beating New Zealand in the only Test in Christchurch, 17-3.

In 1922, the New Zealanders sent two teams—the Maoris in July and the All Blacks in August. The Maoris toured the NSW country centres and drew large mid-week crowds of over 10 000. In 1923, the NSWRU were so impressed with the Maori team that they invited them back again.

So crucial were these few years to rugby union in Australia that in 1986 the Australian Rugby Union retrospectively awarded Test status to all matches played by NSW against other countries.

Dr. Herbert Moran, Captain of the 1908 Wallabies, President of the Balmain and Glebe-Balmain Clubs and International Rugby Board representative, was of the strong view that the game of rugby union may well have disappeared forever if it had not survived in NSW, and that it would not have survived in NSW if it had not been for the leadership of the returning AIF players and officials.

There is, therefore, a case that all the prominence which rugby union now enjoys in Australia and on the world stage may never have come to pass without the emergence of that great 1919 AIF Rugby Union Squad.

The Players

Bruce 'Jackie' Beith

Bruce McNeil Beith was born in Mudgee, New South Wales, on 28 September 1893—one of five children born to Robert and Edith Beith. He was educated at Mudgee Grammar and then at Barker College, Hornsby, where he played rugby in the 1909 and 1910 1st XV teams. He matriculated in 1910 and then completed his Bachelor of Medicine and Master of Surgery at the University of Sydney in 1916.

Barker College rugby was in its infancy when Beith first played for the school but he developed enough talent and skill to not only play for St Andrew's College but to be selected as the fullback for the University of Sydney 1st XV in 1913. He earned two University Blues and also played for the Eastern Suburbs Rugby Football Club.

In 1913 Beith earned a place in the NSW State team and in 1914, only a few weeks after the outbreak of the First World War in Europe, he was selected for the Australian team to play in the Third Test against New Zealand at the Sydney Sports Ground on 15 August 1914 (Wallaby number 145).

On completion of his medical degree he worked briefly at the Repatriation Hospital in Randwick (now the Prince of Wales) before enlisting on 14 July 1916 as a Captain with the Australian Army Medical Corps (AAMC). Beith embarked from Australia on 8 November 1916 and initially served at the No. 1 Australian General Hospital at Rouen, France from 21 January 1917.

On 6 March 1917 he was transferred to the 15th Australian Field Ambulance. A few weeks later on 16 April 1917 he was transferred to the 57th Battalion which was involved in the Battle of Polygon Wood in September 1917 and Villiers-Bretonneaux in April 1918. He was transferred once again to the 53rd Battalion in August 1918 which took part in the capture of Mont St. Quentin and Péronne and the Battle of St. Quentin Canal.

Beith was mentioned in Sir Douglas Haig's Despatches on 1 October 1918 for his 'gallant and efficient services' during the battle of Péronne and the Hindenburg Offensive. The despatch read:

> This officer performed gallant and efficient service as R.M.O. to the 53rd Australian Battalion during the period July to October including the battles of Péronne and Morlancourt and the attack on the Hindenberg Line at Bellicourt. The officers of the battalion speak with highest admiration of his work throughout this period. In the attack on the Hindenberg Line near Bellicourt on October 1st 1918 Captain Beith successfully organised the work of dressing and evacuating wounded of his battalion under heavy shell fire though more than half of his A.M.C. details and ambulance personnel attached to him had been killed or wounded. This Officer has also rendered extremely good service with the 57th Battalion A.I.F. and the 15th Australian Field Ambulance.'

Beith was selected to play for the AIF Trench Team match against the French Army on 19 January 1919. Beith was also selected to play fullback for the AIF First XV and played in four of the five King's Cup matches. Beith considered the AIF versus New Zealand game in Bradford to be the best match he ever played in, for the simple reason that this was the only game he would play against New Zealand in which they sustained a defeat. After the game against Canada, Beith met the Prince of Wales and Prince Albert.

Immediately after the war Beith stayed in England to further his studies at the University of St Andrews. Returning to Australia in February 1920 he was selected for the New South Wales (Australia) side to play in the 1920 Test Series against New Zealand in Sydney. Even though New Zealand remained undefeated in the three Tests, Beith was described as the best player on the field in the Second Test and earned high praise for his performance as fullback during the series.

Beith retired from representative rugby soon after and became a full-time General Practitioner. In 1924 he moved to Gunnedah where he married a local girl, Bess Goodwin, and had three children. In the early

1930's he relocated to Brisbane, before finally moving to Uralla, NSW, in the late 1930's where he practiced as a General Practitioner for the rest of his life. He provided the town with a full range of medical services and also sometimes acted as the local vet. His first wife Bess died in 1941, and in 1948 he remarried.

Throughout his life, Beith always maintained a keen interest in rugby. He was involved with the re-formation of Queensland Rugby Union in 1928 and for a time was a selector in NSW and Queensland. He always attended the major games in Sydney with his rugby friends, especially when the French team was touring. In August 1961 he travelled from his home in Uralla to watch Australia play France at the Sydney Cricket Ground for the last time. He was staying with friends in his usual suites at The Australia Hotel when he suffered a fatal heart attack after the game. Beith is buried at the Northern Suburbs Crematorium in Sydney.

John 'Plumb' Bond

John Herbert Bond was born in 1892 at Newcastle, NSW, to Robert John Bond and Harriet Ann Dennett. After graduating from Wickham Public School, Newcastle Bond played for North Newcastle that won the 1910 and 1911 Newcastle premierships. An enthusiastic hooker, Bond played with determination and tenacity.

Working as a carpenter, Bond enlisted in the AIF on 18 July 1915 as a private and was assigned to the B Company, 30th Battalion. He embarked on 9 November 1915 and the 30th Battalion's first major battle was at Fromelles, France, in July 1916. During the course of the war he was promoted through the ranks and became the B Company Quartermaster Sergeant.

The 30th Battalion fought its last major action of the war when it was involved in the attack on the Hindenburg Line across the top of the St Quentin Canal tunnel. It was during this action that Bond earned the Meritorious Service Medal. The recommendation read:

> This N.C.O. has rendered very valuable service to his company during the period 16-17th Sept and 31st Dec 1918-1st Jan 1919. He has served continuously with his [company] during the whole period and whether in or out of the line, he has displayed untiring energy

and great zeal in his many duties with his unit. During the attack on the Hindenburg Line near Bellicourt in September when his [company] was in the front line he performed a very fine feat of organisation in the distribution of hot food and rations to members of his unit in a position which was being very heavily shelled by the enemy. The benefit derived by the tired troops from this hot food cannot be overestimated and the success of its delivery was mainly due to this N.C.O. An original member of the Battalion, this N.C.O. has held his present rank for nearly two years, and the high sense of duty displayed by him at all times cannot be spoken of too highly.

Bond was selected to play for the AIF Trench Team in the match against the French Army on 19 January 1919. Bond was also selected for the AIF First XV and played in four of the five King's Cup matches. On the AIF Team's Australia Tour Bond played in all eight matches; one of only two players to do so - the other being Thomas 'Tom' Stenning.

After his discharge, Bond joined the Glebe-Balmain Rugby Football Club and played 16 games for New South Wales. In 1920, he made his international debut against New Zealand (Wallaby number 148). He appeared in all three Tests played at Sydney Sports Ground. Australia lost the matches 15-26, 6-14 and 13-24. He managed to score a try in the second Test through his determination and support play.

Bond made the tour of New Zealand in 1921 and played eight out of ten matches including a sole Test at

Christchurch, which Australia won 17 to nil. Australia lost only the last match of the tour to Wellington 8 to 16.

Bond married Mary Lillian Bond and lived and worked in the Newcastle area until his death on 17 September 1963, aged 71.

James 'Jimmy' Bosward

James Hamilton Bosward was born in Paddington, Sydney, in December 1889 to William George Bosward and Isabella Hamilton Browne. Little is known of Bosward's early life but he had good sporting ability as in 1910 at the age of 21 he was playing for Eastern Suburbs Rugby Union Club. He was a fast centre-half forward and was named in media reports for his dash and penetrating style of play, often not having the back up support to finish off his bursting runs. Bosward earned two caps playing for the New South Wales in 1913.

Bosward was working as a bank manager at the outbreak of the First World War and he lost a brother, Charles Frederick Richmond Bosward at Gallipoli on 14 August 1915. This news must have troubled Bosward who subsequently enlisted in the AIF on 29 April 1916 as a gunner and allocated to the Australian Field Artillery. He embarked on 14 September 1916 and disembarked at Plymouth on 2 November 1916. He spent three months at the Parkhouse Artillery Training Depot and was shipped to France from Folkestone on the 28 February 1917.

Taken on strength with the 1st Field Artillery Brigade on 13 March 1917 he was transferred on 13 May 1917 and taken on strength with the 5th Field Artillery Brigade. Over the next three months Bosward was admitted to hospital twice with no wound or sickness listed, however whatever the health problem it was serious enough to be taken back to the UK on 2 August 1917 and admitted to the Oxford Hospital.

Bosward rejoined his unit in France three months later on 17 November 1917. He was taken on strength with the 14th Battery, 5th Field Artillery Brigade on 2 December 1917. Within a few weeks Bosward became incapacitated and was again sent back to the UK suffering from trench foot. He took some six months to recuperate and returned to his unit in France on 10 July 1918 and was taken back on strength on 11 September 1918.

Bosward was selected to play for the AIF Trench Team match against the French Army on 19 January 1919. Bosward was also selected for the AIF First XV and played in two of the five King's Cup matches. On the AIF Team's Australia Tour Bosward played in seven of the eight matches.

Bosward was demobilised on 12 August 1919 and he married Alice Margery Wearne on 15 September 1920 at Marrickville, NSW.

After the war he returned to work as a bank manager and worked in Casino, Lithgow and Parkes. After retiring in 1958 he travelled with his wife on a three month long tour of the UK. Bosward died at Sutherland, NSW on the 21 November 1962, aged 74.

William 'Roger' Bradley

William Roger Bradley was born in March 1893 at Botany, NSW, to Father James Bradley.

Working as a commercial traveller Bradley enlisted in the AIF as a private on 26 July 1915 and was allocated to the 13th Battalion. He embarked on 30 September 1915.

Bradley was selected for the AIF First XV and played in four of the five King's Cup matches. On the AIF Team's Australia Tour Bradley played in seven of the eight matches.

Bradley married Ruby May Pemberton in 1919 at Redfern. From 1932 to 1963 William and his wife lived at the family home at 16 Pretoria Parade, Hornsby. He was listed as a clerk in 1932 and from 1937 to his death as a salesman. Bradley died in 1965 at Balmain aged 72. He had no children.

Peter Buchanan

Peter Neave Buchanan was born on 11 January 1889 in Wellington, New Zealand, to J.C. Buchanan. Buchanan was educated and completed a carpentry apprenticeship in New Zealand before moving to Australia. Little is known about his rugby career prior to the war.

Working as a joiner, Buchanan enlisted in the AIF on 18 September 1915 as an acting Sergeant and assigned to the 19th Battalion. Arriving in France in early 1916, the 19th Battalion took part in the last battle of Pozieres and the defence of Flers-Courcelette, France. The 19th Battalion took part in many battles on the Western Front, including the second Bullecourt, Menin Road, Poelcappelle and the legendary attack on Mont St Quentin. Montbrehain was the battalion's last battle before it was disbanded in 1918. Through the course of the war Buchanan was promoted to Company Sergeant Major.

The casualties of 1918, combined with long-term leave for 1914 enlistees, and dwindling new enlistments sapped the strength of the AIF. On 10 October 1918 the 19th Battalion was disbanded to reinforce other battalions in the brigade. Buchanan was transferred to the 3rd Battalion.

Buchanan was selected to play for the AIF Trench Team match against the French Army on 19 January 1919 and captained the team. Buchanan was also selected to play for the AIF First XV and played in the first of the five King's Cup matches. After this Buchanan captained the AIF Reserve Team. Buchanan played in seven of the eight matches of the AIF Team's Australia Tour at five-eight.

After the war Buchanan played for the Glebe-Balmain Rugby Football Club. He did not get a run against the New Zealand side of 1920, but he appeared for the Metropolitan team against the 1921 Springboks, captaining the side and kicking two conversions. It was a decent showing by the metropolitan team, being narrowly defeated by 8 to 14.

Buchanan did not get a run against the 1922 All Blacks but he did get on the field in the second NSW match against the 1923 Maori tourists. He came on as a replacement when 'Pup' Raymond was injured. 'Pup' Raymond and Billy Sheehan were unable to play in the third NSW match (won 14-12 by the Blues). Buchanan started in the game, as a centre with 'Bot' Stanley. This match was the highlight of his representative career. In all, he played in two international Tests but his name is not listed in *The encyclopaedia of New Zealand Rugby* as New Zealand has never approved the Maori games as Test matches, whereas Australia has.

Buchanan also played for New South Wales seven times between 1919 and 1923. He married Winifred Arnet in 1922 in Sydney. He worked as a carpenter and lived in Sydney until he died in 1957.

Daniel 'Danny' Carroll

Daniel Brendan Carroll was born on 17 November 1887 at Flemington, Victoria. His family moved to Sydney during his childhood. He was a 'quicksilver' runner who was clocked in the 100 yard events as a schoolboy. Carroll played rugby for St Aloysius College in Sydney from 1903 to 1905 and with the St George Club from 1906 to 1908. Recognising Carroll's talent as a winger, the experienced St George and Australian forward Harold Judd took the youngster under his wing. In 1908 Carroll made the State side against Queensland and the touring Anglo-Welsh team.

Carroll's performances for NSW against Queensland and the Anglo-Welsh team in his first representative year won him selection for Australia's inaugural national rugby team to tour the northern hemisphere—the 1908-09 Australia Rugby Union tour of the British Isles and France. The Australian team, which became known as the Wallabies, did not play in the now traditional green-and-gold colours, but wore light-blue jerseys with a Waratah on the left breast. Carroll was the youngest member of the tour squad at 20 years not to mention the fastest (Wallaby number 93). Carroll played as a winger in the first Test of the tour, the 6-9 loss to Wales at Cardiff Arms Park which was the first rugby Test played by an Australian team on British soil.

The 1908-09 tour coincided with the London Olympic Games in which rugby union was an event. Initially the 1908 Olympic organisers expected three teams but reigning champions France withdrew, leaving the touring Wallabies to play Cornwall, the Champion English team, representing England in a one-off match. The Australian team won the gold medal easily by defeating England 32-3 (Carroll scored two tries) and each Wallaby in the match against Cornwall became Olympic gold medallists. In all, Carroll scored 15 tries in the 31 matches of the tour.

In 1912, Carroll was selected for the Australian Rugby Union tour of Canada and the USA. The American newspapers, aware of Australia's Olympic gold medal for rugby, dubbed the visitors 'the world champions of rugby' but the tour was a disappointment with the squad billeted out in college fraternity houses where the hospitality played havoc with team discipline. As a result the team initially lost against two California University sides and three Canadian provincial sides but rose to the occasion for the sole Test of the tour—the November 1912 clash against the United States at Berkeley, winning 12-8. Carroll played at fly-half in that match and scored a try. Carroll thus made two Test career appearances for Australia.

Carroll stayed on in California and enrolled at Stanford University to study geology. He was on the Stanford rugby team for four years and won his letter in rugby in 1913, 1914 and 1915. He played for All-America against the All Blacks in 1913, a Test won by New Zealand 51-3.

During the First World War Carroll served in the U.S. Army as a First Lieutenant in the 364th Regiment, 91st Division, American Expeditionary Force. He was sent to France where on 28 September 1918 he was awarded the Distinguished Service Cross for his leadership. The citation read:

> The Distinguished Service Cross is presented to Daniel B. Carroll, First Lieutenant, U.S. Army, for extraordinary heroism in action near Bois de Cheppy, France, September 28, 1918. Although wounded in the arm in the attack of September 26, Lieutenant Carroll gallantly led his platoon forward, under heavy artillery and machinegun fire, through the Bois de Cheppy. Later, while leading his platoon in an attack near Neuve Grange Farm, he continued on until severely wounded a second time.

Despite recovering from his wounds Carroll was 'co-opted' into the AIF First XV in 1919 and played two matches in the King's Cup against Canada and New Zealand.

After the war Carroll completed his degree in geology at Stanford University and was coaching rugby at the university when he was selected as the playing coach of the USA side for the 1920 Antwerp Olympics.

The first Wallaby shirt was a light shade of blue, rather than the golden yellow currently used by the Australian team. The motif is the crimson Waratah.

At the 1908 London Olympics the Australians utilized his speed by playing him in the centre, but at the 1920 Antwerp Olympics Carroll himself decided, as player-coach, to play in the scrum-half position where his tactical knowledge could be put to its best use. The Americans won the gold and Carroll won his second Olympic gold medal in rugby.

After Stanford, Carroll furthered his education at Oxford University and the Royal School of Mines in England. In 1921, he took up an appointment with Standard Oil in the US and remained with the company until his retirement.

Carroll played his last game of rugby in 1921 when a pick-up team visited British Columbia. His non-playing rugby career continued when in 1924 he coached the gold-medal winning USA Rugby Team at the 1924 Paris Olympics.

Carroll married Helen Warden from Great Falls, Montana, in 1927 and they had one son, Daniel. Helen died in 1941 and Carroll remarried. For the last 35 years of his life Carroll worked for Standard Oil in Great Falls, Montana, Denver, Colorado and New Orleans, Louisiana. At the time of his death he was a tax and insurance commissioner for the company and lived in Kenner, New Orleans.

Carroll died on 5 August 1956 in New Orleans, Louisiana. After his death some of his rugby mementos were sent back to relatives in Australia. One of his Olympic gold medals is currently kept in a Sydney bank vault.

The 1908 London Olympics gold medal for rugby.

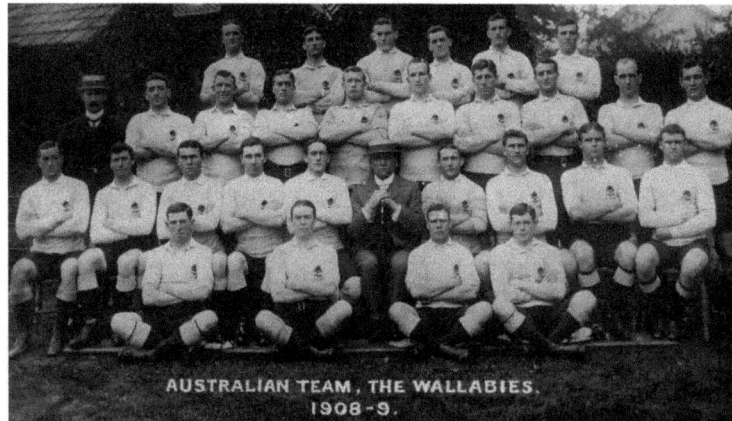

The Australia rugby union team on its first rugby union tour of the British Isles, circa 1908.

Back row, left to right: Thomas Griffen, Ward Prentice, Daniel Carroll, Arthur McCabe, Joseph Stevenson, Phil Carmichael.

3rd row, left to right: Stan Wickham (assistant manager), Peter Flanagan, Charles McMurtrie, Peter Burge, Patrick McCue, Sydney Middleton, Frank Smith, Tom Richards, Norm Row, Robert Craig.

2nd row, left to right: Esmond Parkinson, Christopher McKivatt, Edward Mandible, E. McIntyre, Herbert Moran (captain), James McMahon (manager), Fred Wood (vice-captain, Jumbo Barnett, Charles Hammond, Charles Russell.

Front row, left to right: Jack Hickey, Malcolm McArthur, William Dix, H. Daly.

The Australian 1908 London Olympics side.

The Australian side than played the USA on 16 November 1912.

1 Wogan, 2 Adamson, 3 George, 4 Fraser, 5 Jones, 6 Meibusch, 7 Flynn, 8 R. Hill, 9 Fahey, 10 Wylie, 11 Pugh, 12 Kent, 13 Murphy, 14 Dwyer, 15 Messenger, 16 Griffin, 17 Ward Prentice (Captain), 18 Dr Bohrsman (Manager), 19 Richards (Vice-Captain), 20 D. Carroll, 21 W.W. Hill, 22 Walker, 23 Cunningham, 24 Watson, 25 Tasker, 26 Dunbar, 27 Clarken.

The 1914 Leland Stanford Junior University side

1. Watkins, 2. Blase, 3. Maloney, 4. Gard, 5. Clover, 6. Wilcox, 7. Urban, 8. Wines, 9. Austin , 10. Carroll, 11. Brown, 12. Lachmund, 13. Davidson, 14. Darsie, 15. Peck, 16. Andrews, 17. Erb, 18. Hall, 19. Reeves, 20. Tilton.

The USA side that played New Zealand in 1913

Back Row (L-R): Daniel Brendon Carroll (Stanford University), Clark Lewis Boulware (not used) (Stanford University), Haley (not used) (Stanford University), William Pettigrew Darsie (Stanford University), Herbert Rowell Stolz (replacement) (Stanford University), Brant (?) or Flemming (not used) (?), Joseph C. Urban (Stanford University), A. Knowles (replacement) (?), Charles A. Austin (Olympic), G. Voight (Santa Clara University), Frank Jacob Gard (Captain) (Stanford University), Roland Roy Blase (Stanford University), William Norris King (University of California).

Front Row: Forbes (not used) (?), Stirling Benjamin Peart (University of California), Joseph Louis McKim (University of California), G. Glasscock (Olympic), E.B. Hall (Stanford University), Benjamin Edward Erb (not used) (Stanford University), zLouis Cass (Stanford University), Mowatt Merrill Mitchell (Los Angeles Athletic Club), Quill (not used) (Santa Clara), J.A. Ramage (Santa Clara University).

James 'Jimmy' Clarken

James C. Clarken was born on 19 July 1876 at Thames, New Zealand, to Father P. Clarken and came to Australia as a teenager. Clarken was a robust forward who first played with the Glebe Club in 1900 when it won the Sydney District Premiership in all three grades. He made the first of his 24 appearances for NSW against Queensland in 1904. His speed around the paddock and great ball skills saw him selected in the Australian team... for the backrow! Clarken's Wallaby debut was for the Test against New Zealand in Dunedin on 2 September 1905 (Wallaby number 65), which New Zealand won 14 to 3. He played as a prop in three more Tests in 1910 against New Zealand.

Clarken toured North America with the Australian side led by Ward Prentice in 1912 but missed out on playing the Test against the USA at Berkeley, California, which Australia won 12 to 8. In all he received four international caps and played a club record of 140 games for Glebe, ending his career with 11 games for Randwick. A month before the tour Clarken and Harold Baker, a fellow Australian rugby international and life saver, brought eight surfers ashore at Maroubra Beach in one of Australia's most famous mass rescues and was awarded the Albert Medal.

At age 38 and employed as a motor mechanic Clarken enlisted in the AIF on 26 April 1915, the day after the landings at Gallipoli. He was assigned as a private to the 3rd Australian General Hospital. He embarked just three weeks later on 15 May 1915.

Clarken served with the 3rd Australian General Hospital on Lemnos Island, Greece from August 1915. In a letter home Clarken wrote: 'We have no tents to live in yet, although here four weeks. We are living in the open, on the side of a big hill, and it is very nice of a night time, only fresh water is scarce, and we are all wondering what it would be like to have a wash with a bit of soap and unlimited water. I am keeping fine and dandy, and have only been down one day so far; but some of our chaps are feeling it. I am sorry I did not have more time in England. If I live this thing through I will revisit it, I think, and see some of the football heads.'

In October 1915 Clarken wrote: 'Your very welcome letter to hand. I am grateful for news of the rugby union and good old Sydney. I receive *The Referee* [magazine] and other papers regularly, and see all the news, and, of course, the R.U. Notes are always first read. I am very pleased to see the game is still going, as it is for the right purpose, and I always read with delight the names who have answered the call. Gee, it makes one think and bite his lip; still, enough said. Like you, I regret the departure of such men as George and Thomas, and 'Blair I.' [Swannell] besides many others too numerous to mention. However, we will still keep having a go.'

Clarken was evacuated with enteric fever to Malta and later wrote:

> Still on deck, although in my ninth week of hospital, have touch of enteric fever, and I heard afterwards I was nearly a "goner." I am in Malta now, and doing well, although a bit weak in the legs. Eating well, and feeling otherwise fine and dandy. Before leaving Lemnos met Sid Middleton and Billy Watson; in fact, met a host of footballers, and saw a few good games. Played in one myself, but owing to fever missed the others. Captain Walter Matthews is playing a great game for our side. Tom Richards plays with the 1st Field Ambulance. The daddy of them all is the [New] Zealand section. They had nine men who had worn their black, and included E. Roberts and F. Wilson. We had some talent at Lemnos in the rugby line. The place here is most interesting, and I am seeing all I can. They must have the finest churches in the world. They have some funny customs, such as the milkman parading the streets with his goats from door to door. No cows employed. One has to get off the footpath to let them pass along. We see all shipping come and go from this port, and as it is 10 times more than in the case of Sydney, you may guess it is interesting.

After time in Malta, Clarken was sent back to Australia to recover. He was then transferred to the 4th Motor Transport Company. The role of the Motor Transport was to provide all transport between railhead and divisional trains in order to get supplies forward.

Clarken arrived in France in 1916, where the 4th Motor Transport Company was at the Somme in time for the first battle of Bullecourt, Ypres, the defence of Amiens and the battle of Hamel.

At age 43 Clarken was selected to play for the AIF Trench Team in the match against the French Army on 19 January 1919. Clarken was also selected for the AIF First XV but only played in the King's Cup match against New Zealand. He persuaded the selectors to play him as hooker in this crucial match against the unbeaten New Zealand team that included six All Blacks. The rumour has it that he said, 'I know how to beat the New Zealanders!' In those days New Zealand was persisting with a two-man front row. Clarken's tactic was to stick his head in between them and secure the loose head prop for the AIF no matter which side the ball was put in. On the AIF Team's Australia Tour Clarken played three of the eight matches.

After the war he ran a car-hire business in the Randwick area. Clarken died on 31 July 1953 in Sydney just after his 77th birthday.

Ernest 'Bill' Cody

Ernest Austin Stanislaus Cody was born at Clifton Hill, Victoria, in March 1892. His family moved to Sydney where Cody attended St Patrick's College and later St Joseph's College at Hunters Hill, Sydney. He acquired the nick name 'Bill' because of the fame at the time of 'Buffalo Bill' Cody in the United States. Cody was tall for his age and played rugby for St Joseph's College as a flanker.

Working as a clerk/customs assistant at Custom House and playing for Eastern Suburbs Cody was selected to play for Australia in 1913. Cody was not unusual in that he played for Australia before he had represented his State, nor even for the fact that he never pulled on a New South Wales jersey in his career, but most players who emulated those feats played little part in their tour's main matches and certainly they would be second-stringers in a country like New Zealand. Not so Cody, who was one of the hardest-worked members of the 1913 Wallabies across the Tasman (Wallaby number 125). After missing the tour opener Cody became one of the integral members of the side that improved as the tour went on, finally defeating the All Blacks in the third Test after suffering heavy reverses in the first two.

The Wallabies had an exceptionally difficult start to the tour, as they began against Auckland, who had just lost the Ranfurly Shield after eight years, and then played Taranaki, the new holders. A narrow loss was sustained in the first match and a narrow win recorded in the second, while an unexpected if small defeat was the tourists' lot at Wanganui. It did not bode well for the first Test, especially as the heavy grounds encountered had not been to the visitors' liking and there was sure to be another in the international. It was actually far worse; the match was played in a southerly storm with torrential rain and not even the dreadful weather could keep the All Blacks from running up a 30-5 margin before the main team left for California. To this stage of the tour Cody, along with the other forwards in the team, had been required to 'dig it in', but often when going backwards. Unless that problem could be countered, the tour promised to be a long and not very distinguished one.

Australia's forwards did improve and the loose trio—normally Cody, Fred Thompson and Paddy Murphy—became more prominent. Although the next two matches were also lost, to traditional tough nut Southland and the second Test against a completely new All Black side, Australia made a success of the last fortnight and won the final three matches, including the third Test in a match where the Wallaby loose forwards were particularly prominent. Cody returned home with three international caps as one of the success stories of

a team that fared rather better than many expected. On return to Australia, Cody moved to Randwick in 1914 when this club was promoted to the first division, but he was not selected to play against the All Blacks in their 1914 tour.

Cody enlisted in the AIF on 5 January 1916 and was allocated to the 7th Field Artillery Brigade as a gunner. He embarked on 11 May 1916 and after some additional training in England proceeded with his unit to France on 29 December 1916. After several months in the field Cody was selected in August 1917 to attend the Artillery Cadet School at St John's Wood, UK. He graduated and was promoted to 2nd Lieutenant in February 1918. In March he returned to his unit at Rouelle, France and on 7 May 1918 was promoted to 1st Lieutenant.

Cody was selected to play for the AIF Trench Team in the match against the French Army on 19 January 1919. Cody was also selected for the AIF First XV and played in all five of the King's Cup matches. On the AIF Team's Australia Tour, Cody played the first four matches but injured his leg in the match against Queensland. With no chance of recovery, he left the tour and was discharged from the AIF on 19 August 1919.

After the war, Cody settled in Sydney and worked as a public servant. He married Lucy Florence Fahey in Chatswood in 1928. They spent their entire married lives at 24 Killara Avenue, Gladesville. Lucy died in 1962, and Cody died on 30 December 1968.

Vivian 'Viv' Dunn

Vivian Alphonsus Dunn was born in 1895 in Junee, New South Wales, to father Timothy Dunn. Growing up he played rugby locally as an all-round forward.

Working as a carpenter, Vivian Dunn enlisted on 16 October 1916 and served as a Sapper with the 1st Field Company Engineers. The field engineers were responsible for the construction of bridges, roads, tunnels, trenches, communication lines and buildings of all kinds. He embarked on 10 May 1917 and arrived on the Western Front the next month.

Dunn saw action at Menin Road, Polygon Wood, Passchendaele and Hazebrouck. Dunn was promoted to Lance Corporal and on 25 August 1918, during the Battle of Amiens, he received a recommendation for 'bravery and efficiency under fire.' The recommendation read:

> During the attack on 23rd [Aug] a strong point was commenced on the objective under heavy shell and close MG fire. L/Cpl Dunn undertook the wiring of this position. He commenced detaching enemy existing wire, dragging it into position and erecting it. He did not hesitate or cease until the job was properly done. He shows a fine example to his comrades and greatly assisted in the quick consolidation of the post. He is recommended for bravery and efficiency under fire.'

There is no record, however, whether the recommendation was approved or that any award was made to Dunn.

Dunn was selected to play for the AIF Trench Team match against the French Army on 19 January 1919. Dunn was also selected to play for the AIF First XV and played in four of the five King's Cup matches. Dunn played in seven of the eight matches of the AIF Team's Australia Tour.

Dunn's international rugby career began in 1920 against the visiting All Blacks where he played in all three Tests (Wallaby number 151). He was the first representative player from Junee, Southern Districts of NSW, and played at number eight in all three Tests against the visiting New Zealand side in Sydney in 1920.

In 1921 he moved to Sydney and joined the Glebe-Balmain Club. The club was originally formed in 1919 as Glebe-Balmain RUFC by players from the old Balmain and Glebe Rugby Clubs. These players wished to continue playing Rugby after most of their club-mates opted to join the newly-formed Glebe and Balmain rugby league clubs in 1909. The name changed to Drummoyne District RUFC in 1930.

Dunn played against the South African tourists in Sydney in 1921. Although Australia lost the three matches against the South Africans, the following month's tour of New Zealand was a different proposition. Australia won nine of 10 games including a notable 17 to nil victory over New Zealand by scoring four tries to nil. Dunn showed his all-round skills in the lineouts, mauls and rucks during the Test win. He played seven minor games during the tour and captained against Waikato and scored a try against Bay of Plenty.

In all, Dunn played in seven Tests for Australia and was in seven non-Test matches. He captained Australia once, but not in a Test. He also played 15 Tests for New South Wales between 1919 and 1921.

It is unknown when he died.

Stephen 'Pat' Egan

Egan was selected for the AIF First XV and played in three of the five King's Cup matches. On the AIF Team's Australia Tour Egan played in one of the eight matches.

Alma 'Ray' Elliott

Alma Raymond Elliott was born in 1897 at Sydney to Rose Elliott. He played as a flanker with South Sydney and Glebe-Balmain.

Working as a carpenter, Elliott enlisted in the AIF as a private on 15 April 1915 and was allocated to the 3rd Australian General Hospital. He embarked on 15 May 1915 and was transferred to the 5th Field Ambulance. The 5th Field Ambulance landed with the 5th Brigade on Gallipoli as medical support for the 17th, 18th, 19th and 20th Battalions. The unit landed on the peninsula on 21 August 1915 and participated in the closing stages of the August Offensive, including the attack at Hill 60. The role of the Field Ambulance was the evacuation of casualties from the battlefields, or from regimental aid posts to field ambulances. They were trained to administer basic first aid so that casualties could be hand carried to aid posts for further treatment. They often had to make decisions about what priority casualties were given or whether those with grievous wounds with little chance of survival would be evacuated at all.

After the withdrawal from Gallipoli in December 1915, the 5th Field Ambulance regrouped in Egypt before sailing for the Western Front. They arrived in time for the battles of the Somme, Passchendaele, Polygon Wood and Pozières in 1916. The 5th Field Ambulance continued to serve along the Western Front, culminating in the battle of Amiens on 8 August 1918.

Elliott was selected for the 1919 AIF Squad and played for the AIF Reserve Team.

Unlike many fine sportsmen, whose careers (and often lives) were wrecked or ended by the war, Elliott returned from the conflict ready to take his place as one of Australia's leading forwards of the early 1920s. Hardened both physically and mentally, he was soon to become one of the indispensable men in the Waratahs pack and the team never looked as strong without him. At 6ft (1.83m) and 13 stone (83kg), he was one of the bigger men in the New South Wales pack of his day and he used his size and strength well.

Elliott was included as lock in the first Test team chosen to face the 1920 All Blacks (Wallaby number 152). Although New South Wales suffered a 15-26 defeat, which did not please the critics or selectors, the quality of the performance was not initially appreciated. This All Black side was extremely good—they were the last team from New Zealand to return unbeaten until 1938—and they created all kinds of scoring records on tour. Elliott was one axed after the first Test, to be replaced by Geoff Wyld and then Watty Friend.

Elliott's only appearance against the 1921 Springboks was for Metropolitan Union but he was chosen for the New Zealand tour that year, where he made a quick and decisive move to the top. While many of the teams met on the 1921 tour were not those in the top echelon of New Zealand provinces, almost all were country unions who boasted good, hard packs. Elliott began as a back-row forward in the 3-2-3 scrum that New South Wales favoured at the time, but he moved into lock when injuries and a lack of form prompted a reshuffle. While hardly ever singled out for individual praise, Elliott was one of the successes of the tour and his non-stop work ethic was just what the lightweight pack required. The side had talent to burn in the backs, especially in the lightning-fast three-quarters, but that would have been of little use without a good supply of ball.

Soon recognised as one of the team mainstays, Elliott only missed the Bay of Plenty match (the tour's third game) and was chosen at lock for the Test against New Zealand. This match, which New Zealand did not take too seriously—for example they replaced Mullins, the halfback, on the morning of the match and gave the captaincy to Teddy Roberts, the replacement—saw the poorly-prepared home side slaughtered by 17-0, still the heaviest defeat suffered by any New Zealand team at home. All the visitors had exemplary matches and, much to the surprise of the majority of spectators, outplayed the home forwards. The 1921 Waratahs only missed an unbeaten tour when defeated by Wellington in the last match, which was played four days after the Test. In the circumstances that defeat—by the reigning Ranfurly Shield holder—was understandable.

Having proved himself on tour, Elliott became a certainty at home. He played the first two matches of the exciting 1922 series against the Maoris but an injury sustained in the second match forced him to leave the field. His replacement, Reg Ferguson, took the vacant place in the thrilling decider that the visitors won 23-22 after being behind 6-22 at halftime. Elliott had recovered by the time a full All Black side arrived three weeks later and New South Wales, after losing the first match,— Elliott this time replaced Ferguson during the game— turned in two excellent games to win the series. Both times the wins were based on a superior effort by the pack, which nullified the New Zealanders' greater weight and height, not to mention non-stop commitment. In both matches the entire pack was praised as a collective unit rather than as individuals, with every man doing his share.

Elliott was an ever-present in the 1923 Maori series —this one, like its predecessor, contained three high-scoring, close matches but the Waratahs won in a sweep. The home forwards employed bustling tactics against the much heavier Maori pack, endeavouring to play the game at high speed. The tactics worked, as none of the matches became a set-piece battle even though rain rendered the pitch muddy and slow for the final contest. Elliott had a good series, being prominent in every match. As one of the limited number of experienced men available for the New Zealand tour and a star for the last three years, he was one of the first chosen for what proved an ill-fated venture.

Without ten of the better players, all of whom were unavailable for one reason or another, and missing six of the chosen team due to university exams that excluded them from the first two matches, the young Waratahs were always going to find this trip hard. Elliott, who played exclusively in the back row on this trip, therefore had a lot on his plate.

He did his work well, winning good notices for his untiring efforts in the tour opener, at Wellington, and capped another strong match at Timaru with his only try for the State—a remarkable statistic for a man who spent so much time on the ball. The Waratahs struggled to contain the much heavier All Black pack in the first Test, although sterling defensive work kept the margin tight. But a week later the tourists, who showed only two changes from the Dunedin match as opposed to New Zealand's eight, copped a heavy defeat at Christchurch. Once again the Blues' pack was overmatched and the loose forwards had to do far too much defending to make any real contribution on attack. Another heavy defeat followed at Napier, when Hawkes Bay-Poverty Bay (in reality the team was mostly drawn from Ranfurly Shield holder Hawkes Bay) followed the same recipe as the All Blacks—using their much heavier forwards to dominate the game before launching back attacks. The result, 32-15, was similar to the Test score as well. Elliott sat the next two matches out—another heavy loss at Auckland was followed by only the second win of the tour at Hamilton—before returning to the fray against an almost new All Black side; there were 14 changes from the Christchurch Test. This time the score was even higher, 38-11, and New South Wales was never in the game. One final match, an average affair that saw Wairarapa-Bush win by 14-8, ended the trip and, as it happened, Elliott's career at the top level. He made one final appearance against an All Black side when he turned out for Metropolitan Union against the 1924 tourists before dropping out of the picture. In all, Elliott played 13 matches representing Australia.

After playing Elliott coached Drummoyne RFC (Glebe-Balmain changed its name)—including to the 1936 Premiership.

Thomas 'Rat' Flannagan

Thomas William Flannagan born in Queensland to Sophia Jane Bradley.

Working as a labourer Flannagan enlisted in the AIF as a private on 7 January 1916 and assigned to the 25th Battalion. He embarked on 31 March 1916.

Flannagan was selected to play for the AIF Trench Team in the match against the French Army on 19 January 1919. Flannagan was also selected for the AIF First XV and played in all five of the King's Cup matches. On the AIF Team's Australia Tour Flannagan played in six of the eight matches.

Munro 'Munnie' Fraser

Munro Fraser was born in 1879 in Auckland, New Zealand, to John Munro Fraser. He was educated in New Zealand and then moved to Sydney.

Fraser was a hard-scrummaging forward who was considered of the same calibre as Jimmy Clarken. He was one of several New Zealanders who played with the Glebe Club in Sydney in the early 1900s. Glebe won seven premierships from the inception of the competition in 1900 to 1914 (1900, 1901, 1906, 1907, 1909, 1912 and 1914). Fraser represented New South Wales eight times between 1909 and 1911, all against Queensland.

He toured the USA and Canada with the Australian team in 1912 at the age of 33. He was the second oldest player on the team after Jimmy Clarken, who was 37. He played in the first tour match against the Barbarians in San Francisco which Australia won 29 to 8. Fraser played a tight defence, chased every loose ball and ultimately scored a try. Fraser played six matches on the tour but unfortunately sustained an injury against the University of California at Berkeley and did not participate for the rest of the tour including the only Test against the USA—he returned to Australia uncapped.

Fraser continued to play for Glebe after the tour; however, he did not play any representative rugby. He helped the Club to win the 1914 premiership before retiring from rugby.

Working as a motor driver Fraser enlisted in the AIF as a private on 16 May 1916 at age of 37 and was allocated to the 4th Reinforcements of the 9th Machine Gun Company (which was later absorbed into the 3rd Machine Gun Battalion). He embarked on 20 October 1916. His unit's first major battle was at Messines, Belgium in June 1917. In September 1917 Fraser was transferred to the 1st Machine Gun Company taking part in the battles of Menin Boad, Passchendaele and Hazebrouck.

He was promoted to Lance Corporal and in March 1918 received a gunshot wound to his leg and forearm. He returned to the front as the Battle of Amiens and the breach of the Hindenburg Line brought an end to the German resistance.

After a bout of influenza, Fraser was selected to coach the AIF Trenches Team which played against the French Army on 19 January 1919.

Fraser returned to Australia on 15 May 1919.

John 'Darb' or 'Jack' Hickey

John Joseph Hickey was born on 4 June 1887 and raised in Glebe, Sydney. He burst onto the Sydney first grade club scene as a 19-year-old three-quarter with Glebe late in the 1906 season. A junior whose talents at once gave promise of being more than an able player, Hickey possessed a good swerving run, 'tricky' traits and was 'a heady player.'

Described by Peter Sharpham in *The First Wallabies* as being 'relatively short in stature, Hickey had powerful, well-developed leg muscles which he used to great effect in evading some of the best defenders in rugby. A brave front-on tackler, he was equally at home in the centres or on the wing.'

Also a steady and reliable short-distance goal kicker, Hickey's combination of tries and goals contributed significantly to the Glebe club as it won back-to-back premierships in 1906 and 1907. In the latter season, Hickey finished in third place on the leading points-scorers' table, just behind Herbert 'Dally' Messenger.

His arrival, though, coincided with the growing turmoil and upheaval caused by the events that led to the formation of rugby league in

Australia. This caused Hickey's career to take numerous unexpected turns, and curtail what may have been a far greater representative rugby union career.

Despite his eye-catching club form, Hickey could not break into the NSW team, and feeling somewhat neglected by the State selectors (and perhaps influenced by older team-mates) in early August 1907 he decided to join the ranks of the newly-formed NSW Rugby League (NSWRL).

Hickey was duly selected in the NSWRL's 'All Blues', and began training with the team in preparation for a three-match series against the New Zealand 'All Golds' professional rugby league team at the Sydney Agricultural Ground.

So taken with the professional movement, Hickey was one of a few select group who were present at the Margaret Street Wharf in Sydney to welcome Albert Baskerville and the All Golds when they arrived in Australia.

After sitting with the NSW All Blues for a team photograph, Hickey (along with Newtown's William Farnsworth) withdrew from the NSWRL and sought to return to rugby union. Despite signing an agreement to play for the League—an act which in itself was enough under the RFUs Rules of Professionalism to warrant an immediate lifetime ban—the NSWRU attributed Hickey's actions to his youthful exuberance, and allowed him to continue his career without penalty. The matter was no longer spoken—seemingly forgotten.

Resuming with Glebe for the 1908 season, Hickey quickly became acclaimed as the State's best centre three-quarter. No longer having to compete with the ubiquitous Herbert 'Dally' Messenger, Hickey played for NSW against Queensland and the touring British (Anglo-Welsh) team.

Hickey duly won selection in the Wallabies team for its inaugural tour of Great Britain (a trip that also extended to France and North America). Disputes though between the home unions over player allowances and professionalism restricted the Australians to tests against England and Wales. Hickey played in both Tests, and was a member of the team that won a gold medal for Rugby Union at the Olympic Games.

Hickey's tour was not without off-field controversy. Even before the Wallabies had sailed out of Sydney, the NSWRU held meetings to decide if Hickey's earlier flirtation with rugby league would pass muster if it was exposed in England during the campaign.

Touring Britain at the same time were J.J. Giltinan and the Kangaroos, and whispers abounded that the All Blues photograph would, via some helpful Australian and English rugby league officials, fall into the hands of the London newspapers and the RFU. The NSWRU satisfied itself that Hickey (and itself) had done nothing wrong, and he duly left with the Wallabies.

Cover-ups by football administrators are apt to unravel, and the photograph duly surfaced. Pressed by the English newspapers for comment, the Wallabies' managers dismissed it as a beat-up. Interviewed by *The Yorkshire Evening Post*, Hickey said his brother had joined the League, hence the confusion. The RFU was satisfied the photo was not of John Hickey and took no action.

After returning home to Australia in August 1909, Hickey was one of the Wallabies who followed the lead of his Glebe team-mate Chris McKivat and defected to rugby league. Hickey was reported to have been given a fee of £100 to take part in three matches between the Wallabies and the Kangaroos.

He performed particularly well in the matches and a reporter for *The Referee* wrote that: 'Hickey has been the most consistent player in each of the games. On form he has no equal—his tackling, running, kicking, and powers in combination being of the highest quality. One wonders what he would be worth to a NU (English Rugby League) club.'

Hickey joined the Glebe Rugby League Club in 1910, and continued to enhance his reputation in the thirteen-man code. He played in a two-Test series against the visiting British team, partnering with Messenger in the centres.

Injury though soon curtailed his representative career and he was unable to regain his form in time to take part in the 1911/12 Kangaroos tour of England. Hickey continued to play on for Newtown (with an interlude at Balmain in 1911), until the outbreak of the First World War.

Working as a labourer and married, John Hickey enlisted on 22 May 1916 as a private and was allocated to the 56th Battalion age 29. He embarked on 7 October 1916 and arrived in France in early 1917—in time for one of Europe's coldest winters. Suffering from frost bite to his left toe, Hickey was evacuated to England, re-joining his Battalion in March 1916. The 56th Battalion's major battles included Polygon Wood, Villers-Bretonneux, and the capture of Péronne. Their last major battle of the war was St Quentin Canal. At some stage during the war Hickey was promoted to Corporal.

Hickey was selected for the AIF First XV and played in three of the five King's Cup matches.

After the war Hickey became a butcher. Hickey's experiences at the war front are said to have so dismayed him that upon returning home he tossed his medals into Sydney Harbour. He was far prouder of his football achievements and Hickey proudly displayed pictorial mementos of his union and league careers for Australia in his Glebe butcher shop.

Hickey remained a popular figure in the then working-class Glebe area, until he died of cancer on 15 May 1950 at the Sacred Heart Hospice, St Vincent's Hospital. He was aged 63 and was survived by his eight children.

Hickey London Olympic Medal and case.

"The Wallabies" who won the Olympic Championship.

T. J. Richards, F. Bede Smith, C. McMurtrie, P. McCue, S. A. Middleton, J. T. Barnett.
F. Roberts (Touch Judge), R. R. Craig, A. J. McCabe, C. H. McKivat (Capt.), J. Hickey, C. Russell, T. Griffin,
M. McArthur, D. B. Carroll, P. Carmichael.

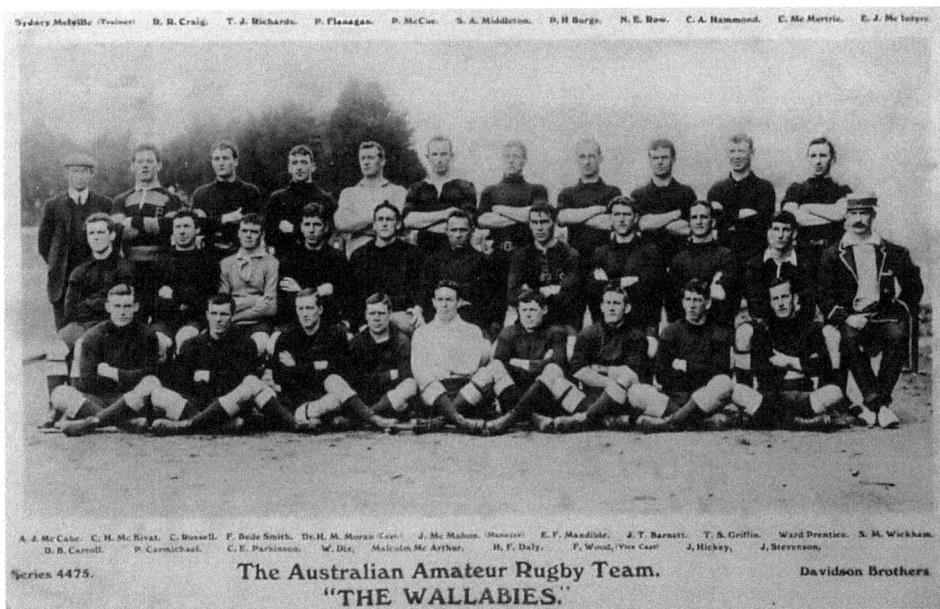

Sydney Melville (Trainer)   B. B. Craig.   T. J. Richards.   P. Flanagan.   P. McCue.   S. A. Middleton.   D. H Burge.   N. E. Row.   C. A. Hammond.   C. Mc Murtrie.   E. J. Mc Intyre.

A. J. McCabe.   C. H. Mc Kivat.   C. Russell.   F. Bede Smith.   Dr. H. M. Moran (Capt.)   J. Mc Mahon. (Manager)   E. F. Mandible.   J. T. Barnett.   T. S. Griffin.   Ward Prentice.   S. M. Wickham.
D. B. Carroll.   P. Carmichael.   C. E. Parkinson.   W. Dix.   Malcolm Mc Arthur.   H. F. Daly.   F. Wood, (Vice Capt)   J. Hickey.   J. Stevenson.

Series 4475.   The Australian Amateur Rugby Team.   Davidson Brothers
                                            "THE WALLABIES."

George Horsey

George Harcombe Horsey was born on 21 April 1892 at Redfern, New South Wales.

Working as a clerk, he enlisted on 8 September 1915 as a gunner and was allocated to the 5th Field Artillery Brigade, embarking on 18 November 1915.

Serving with the 14th Battery, Horsey was wounded at Ypres, Belgium, on 2 October 1917 and invalided to a hospital in Birmingham, England.

On 3 February 1919 Sergeant Horsey was recommended for the Meritorious Service Medal which was subsequently awarded on 6 October 1919. The citation read:

> For most conspicuous gallantry and devotion to duty during the period of the advance from ROISEL to ST. SOUPLET, 17th September, to 20th October, 1918. This N.C.O. was in charge of the ammunition supply. Most of the carting had to be done by night owing to the close proximity of the Battery to the front line, great difficulty being experienced in finding the position owing to the daily moves forward. Throughout the whole operation this N.C.O. showed great initiative and resourcefulness in getting through the many barrages that were encountered, and his sterling example and tactfulness set

to the men under his command resulted in only 8 casualties to animals during the whole period.

Horsey was selected for the AIF Reserve Team and on the AIF Team's Australia Tour where he played in four of the eight matches.

Charles 'Nuggety' Leahey

Charles Walter Leslie Leahey was born at Lithgow, NSW, to James Leahey.

Working as a blacksmith, Leahey enlisted in the AIF as a driver on 7 February 1916 and was allocated to B Company of the 3rd Pioneer Battalion. He embarked on 6 June 1916.

On 26 May 1918 Leahey was recommended for the Military Medal which was awarded on 7 October 1918. The recommendation read:

> On the night of the 25th May, 1918, the ration wagon and water cart were proceeding to "A" Company of this Unit, when a heavy enemy barrage was encountered immediately West of Villers-Bretonneux, near Amiens. Owing to the intense enemy shelling, it was considered inadvisable to send the water cart forward, but as the rations were urgently required, No. 472 Driver Leahey, with absolute disregard for personal safety, volunteered to take the wagon through. This he was successful in doing, at great danger to himself, under the most difficult and exhausting circumstances. [High Explosive] and gas shells were bursting around him, continuously, the wagon being hit in several places. On the return journey, he again showed remarkable courage and fortitude, and it was only by the greatest of good fortune that he escaped personal injury.

Leahey was selected to play for the AIF Trench Team in the match against the French Army on 19 January 1919.

Arthur 'Togo' or 'Budget' Lyons

Arthur Michael Joseph Lyons was born at Cairns, Queensland, to Ellen Lyons.

Working as a sawmill hand, Lyons enlisted in the AIF as a private on 8 April 1916 and was allocated to the 47th Battalion. He embarked on 19 September 1916.

Lyons was selected to play as a forward for the AIF Trench Team in the match against the French Army on 19 January 1919. Lyons was also selected for the AIF First XV and played in four of the five of the King's Cup matches. On the AIF Team's Australia Tour Lyons played in six of the eight matches.

Walter 'Wally' Matthews

Matthews circa 1900

Walter Frederick Matthews was born in 1885 at Macleay River, NSW, to Frederick and Florence Matthews. He was educated at Sydney Grammar School where he was a prefect. Enrolling in 1904, Matthews completed his Bachelor of Medicine and Master of Surgery at St Andrews College, the University of Sydney. He was the captain of the University First XV in 1908 and 1909 and earned two University Blues for rugby and cricket. Matthews played rugby for New South Wales in 1906, 1908 and 1910 and was considered unlucky not to gain selection in the Wallaby team of 1908.

Matthews enlisted in the AIF in Sydney in February 1915 as a Captain with the Australian Army Medical Corps (AAMC). He embarked from Australia on 15 May 1915 and initially served at the No. 3 Australian General Hospital at Mudros in Greece. The unit then served in Abbassia in Egypt, Brighton in England and Abbeville in France. Matthews was promoted to Major on 29 January 1918. From February 1918, Matthews served with the 20th, 42nd and 2nd Casualty Clearing Stations in France.

Group portrait of the medical officers of the 3rd Australian General Hospital grouped in a courtyard at the hospital in Abbassia, Egypt, in July 1916. Matthews is back row third from left. (AWM J01657)

On 1 March 1918, Matthews was recommended for a Distinguished Service Order. The recommendation read:

> At a General Hospital [3ʳᵈ A.G.H.] has been distinguished for his capacity for work, organising ability, initiative, resource and devotion to duty combined with professional skill. During 34 months service, including six months at Lemnos, when during a period of severe stress and strain, owing to the shortage of officers through sickness, Major, then Captain, Matthews worked indefatigably, having for some time 300 patients under his immediate care, including all cerebro-spinal meningitis cases; eight months in Egypt; five in England, and since April 1917 in France, where from September to December 1917, he had charge of a Surgical Division. This Officers' work has been of an exceptionally high standard.

This recommendation was downgraded to a Mention in Despatches which was awarded on 19 September 1918.

In January 1919 the AIF Sports Control Board appointed Matthews as manager and coach of the 1919 AIF Squad. He oversaw the selection, training of the

The 1939 Wallabies pose for a team photograph at Torquay Rugby Ground. Matthews is centre of the middle row.

squad, and the management of the AIF First XV and the AIF Reserve Team as they competed in the Kings' Cup, then completed the AIF Team's Australia tour. During the King's Cup, Matthews pulled on the boots and played at half back in the matches against South Africa and the Royal Air Force.

After the war Matthews moved to Orange, New South Wales, and practised as a General Practitioner. He maintained a close association with rugby and was selected as the Team Manager for the 1933 Wallabies tour of South Africa. This team was generally considered to be the first Australian team to make a tour to a major rugby nation with a truly Australian representation. The team played 23 matches, winning 12, drawing one and losing 10. They caused an upset after early poor form defeating the Springboks in two tests. In 1937 the visiting Springboks played in Orange and South African tour manager, Percy Day, said that on the 1933 tour Matthews proved to be one of the most popular Australia sportsmen to visit South Africa.

Matthews was selected as the Team Manager for the 1939 Wallabies tour of the UK but the day after the team reached Plymouth, Britain declared war on Germany and their tour ended before a ball was kicked in anger.

Matthews served as an Alderman of Orange City Council for 19 years and Mayor from 1936-1944 and 1948-1950. He was one of Orange's most respected sporting administrators, having an enormous influence on both cricket and rugby in the district. Matthews died in 1954.

Matthews circa 1936.

Sydney 'Syd' Middleton

Sydney Albert 'Syd' Middleton was born in Glebe, Sydney, on 24 February 1884. He commenced his rugby career with the Glebe Rugby Club. His first representative appearance was for New South Wales in the interstate series against Queensland in 1908. His performance saw him selected for New South Wales against the touring Anglo-Welsh side of the same year. Middleton was in the right place at the right time and was selected in Australia's inaugural national rugby team to tour the northern hemisphere—Dr Paddy Moran's first Wallabies. The tour was a long one, 36 matches, and Middleton would prove to be a reliable member of the party appearing in 31 of the Wallabies matches. He was the second tallest player in the squad which meant he featured in the Australian line-out. But he was also a robust defender at his physical peak and was selected in every one of the tour's first 18 games.

At the time, the rugby tournament for the London Olympics games may not have appeared to be of great significance. Australia had already beaten Cornwall, the British county champions early in the tour, and Scotland, Ireland and France had all turned down the Rugby Football

Union's invitation to participate in the Olympic bouts. Neither the tour captain Moran, nor the vice-captain Fred Wood played, so Middleton's club captain, Chris McKivat, led the Wallabies to an easy 32-3 victory and to Olympic glory. Each Wallaby in that match thereafter was an Olympic gold medallist.

Middleton made his Test debut on that tour at Rectory Field in Blackheath, NSW—the Test against England in January 1909. Middleton captained New South Wales in matches against the All Blacks and the New Zealand Maori in 1910. That year he also captained the Australian national side in three Tests against the All Blacks, one of which was won. All told, he made 33 national appearances for Australia including four Tests, three as captain.

Middleton retired from rugby in 1911 and concentrated on rowing. He had been a member of the Sydney Rowing Club for some time and regularly appeared in the New South Wales state selection VIII between 1906 and 1911. He contested the 1912 Summer Olympics in the six seat of the Australian eight. The crew won its heat, but lost in a quarter-final to the Leander Club from England that went on to win the gold medal in the eights competition.

Middleton enlisted in the AIF in 1915 as a 2nd Lieutenant with B Company, 19th Battalion, and embarked from Sydney on board HMAT *Ceramic* on 25 June 1915. He served at Gallipoli and in France. He was promoted to Major and posted to the 17th Battalion in

May 1917. Middleton was mentioned in despatches in 1918 and was awarded the Distinguished Service Order in 1919 for bravery in action. His recommendation for the DSO recorded:

> The battalion owes much of its success to the splendid example set by this very fine type of officer. He was in command of the 17th Battalion on the 14th May 1918 east of Heilly, near Amiens, when the enemy made a very determined attack on the front held by the 17th Battalion and the manner in which he handled the situation, and quickly restored the line, showed great initiative and leadership.

After the Armistice, Middleton was integrally involved in arranging sporting events for the Allied troops prior to their demobilisation. In 1920 Middleton was awarded the Order of the British Empire. He died in 1945 in London at 63 years of age.

Joseph Murray

Joseph Murray was born to Matilda Murray.

Working as a cooper in Sydney, Murray enlisted in the AIF as a Lance Corporal on 13 September 1915 and was allocated to the 7th Field Company Engineers. He embarked on 22 December 1915.

For his actions at Bullecourt on 4-5 May 1917, Sergeant Murray was awarded the Distinguished Conduct Medal on 8 November 1917. The recommendation read:

> For conspicuous gallantry and devotion to duty. He displayed great coolness and courage in assisting an officer to mark out and excavate a support trench, moving along the line under intense shell fire to encourage the men.

Later promoted to Company Quarter Master, Sergeant Murray was selected to play for the AIF First XV and played in two of the five King's Cup matches.

William 'Bill' O'Toole

William Charles O'Toole was born at Ryde, New South Wales, to William O'Toole.

O'Toole had eight years' experience as a member of the Lands Department Rifle Club. Working as a licensed surveyor O'Toole enlisted on 10 January 1916 as a Second Lieutenant and was assigned to the 2nd Pioneer Battalion. He embarked on 6 June 1916 and was promoted to Lieutenant in early 1917.

On 27 August 1918, Lieutenant O'Toole was recommended for the Military Cross which was subsequently awarded on 23 May 1919. The citation read:

> For conspicuous gallantry and devotion to duty on 8 August 1918 during the operation East of Amiens. He organised his two platoons so that there was a resourceful party keeping well on the heels of the infantry and recovering trees and wire from the road. He reconnoitred the road under machine gun fire and rifle fire up to where the enemy still held the road at Cerisy. He then actively supervised the work, especially in the vicinity of Gailly Cross where the road was bad and being shelled and fired upon by machine guns from the left flank. He reconnoitred the road between the main Cerisy Road and the river

and carried out his reconnaissance with absolute disregard for the machine guns and snipers shooting at him and later put that road in order, still under fire. His great determination to get the road through inspired his men and it was due to the way he kept his men "sticking it" that over 7 000 yards of road urgently required were thrown open to 18 pounder traffic an hour and a half after zero time.

O'Toole was selected to play as a forward for the AIF Trench Team in the match against the French Army on 19 January 1919. O'Toole was also selected for the AIF Reserve Team and on the AIF Team's Australia Tour he played in six of the eight matches.

Irving 'Irv' Ormiston

Irving William Leonard Ormiston was born on 19 June 1895 at Cowra, New South Wales, to William Faulkner Ormiston. Ormiston attended the Sydney Church of England Grammar School (Shore) in Sydney. After matriculating he played as a flanker for the North-West Rugby Football Club.

Listing his occupation as a wheat farmer, Ormiston enlisted in the AIF on 18 July 1915 as a private and was allocated to the 3rd Infantry Battalion. He embarked on 8 October 1915. The battalion arrived in France in March 1916 and its first major action was at Pozières in July 1916 where Ormiston received a gunshot wound to the abdomen that would keep him out of the action until September.

Moving on to Ypres, Belgium, in October 1916, Ormiston was promoted to 2nd Lieutenant, and then transferred to the Australian 1st Division School of Instruction. Rejoining the unit in March 1917, Ormiston was promoted to First Lieutenant and served with the 5th Battalion.

Ormiston was selected for the 1919 AIF Squad and played in the Reserve Team. Ormiston played in four of the eight matches of the AIF Team's Australia Tour.

After the war Ormiston was selected to play for New South Wales against New Zealand in 1920. He played in all three Tests—Tests that were granted international status in 1986. Ormiston was described as 'a powerful red-headed man of fiery disposition whose unbounded energy delighted spectators.' Ormiston also played four matches for New South Wales.

Ormiston died on 29 August 1969 in London.

Horace 'Dick' Pountney

Horace Randolph Pountney was born on 23 May 1891 at Moree, New South Wales, to Walter Norman Pountney and Elizabeth Whelan. He was educated at the Sydney Church of England Grammar School (Shore) where he captained the rugby First XV.

Pountney was working as a shipping clerk when he enlisted on 14 January 1916 and was assigned to the 26th Battery, 7th Field Artillery Brigade. He embarked on 11 May 1916 as an acting bombardier.

Pountney's younger brother Private Claude Pountney serving with the 7th Light Horse Regiment was killed on 16 August 1915 during the August offensive at Lone Pine, Gallipoli. Pountney's youngest brother, Cyprus Pountney, also served as a gunner with the 7th Field Artillery Brigade.

Pountney was promoted to Second Lieutenant on 19 September 1918 and promoted to First Lieutenant on 19 December 1918. Serving with the 107th Australian Howitzer Battery, 7th Field Artillery Brigade, he was awarded a Mention in Despatches in 24 January 1919.

Pountney was selected for the 1919 AIF Squad and played two games for the AIF First XV in the King's Cup matches against Canada and New Zealand. On the AIF Team's Australia Tour Pountney played in seven of the eight matches.

After the war Pountney lived in Newcastle, New South Wales, and worked as a shipping agent and later a colliery agent. He married Elizabeth Edith Freda Bean in 1924. Pountney died on 9 December 1966 at Newcastle.

Herbert 'Tom' Quinn

Married and working as a tram driver in, Sydney, Quinn enlisted in the AIF as a private on 1 March 1917 and was allocated to the 1st ANZAC Cyclist Battalion. He embarked on 14 June 1917.

Quinn was to play as a forward for the AIF Trench Team in the match against the French Army on 19 January 1919. Quinn was also selected for the AIF First XV and played in three of the five King's Cup matches.

Clifford 'Cliff' Rankin

Clifford Egerton Lore Rankin was born on 4 December 1896 at Geelong, Victoria, to Edwin Walton Rankin. Rankin served for 18 months in the 8th Australian Garrison Artillery before the war.

Working as a plumber he enlisted on 30 December 1915 as a gunner and was allocated to the 5th Siege Artillery Brigade, 36th Heavy Artillery Group and embarked on 9 April 1916.

Rankin was selected for the AIF Reserve Team and on the AIF Team's Australia Tour he played in seven of the eight matches at fullback. Rankin was the only Victorian player in the 1919 AIF Squad.

After the war Rankin returned to Geelong and played Australian Rules Football for Geelong.

Rankin died on 12 February 1975.

Fifth Reinforcements of the Royal Australian Artillery Siege Brigade taken at South Head, Sydney, in March 1916.

Back Row (left to right): Gunners Luff (standing), Woodland, Dalton, Robertson, Powter, Mason, Ion, Gregor, Campbell, Marriott, Paterson (standing).

Second row: Gunners Lewis, Hutton, Bedford, Dangar, White, Gwyther, Desmond, Spencer, O'Shea.

Front row: Gunners Hartman, Wild, Laforest, Harrison, Gell, Rankin, Webber.

(Sydney Mail, *22 March, 1916, p. 17.*)

John Robertson

John Victor Alexander Robertson was born in 1898 at Kelvin Grove, Queensland, to A. Robertson.

Working as a joiner, Robertson enlisted on 18 August 1915 as a driver and was allocated to the 2nd Divisional Ammunition Column. He embarked on 16 November 1915.

Serving with the 104th Howitzer Battery, 4 Field Artillery Brigade, Robertson was recommended for the Military Medal on 31 October 1917 which was subsequently awarded on 27 June 1918. The citations read:

> For conspicuous gallantry and devotion to duty. On the 24th October 1917 near ZONNEBEKE, when carrying ammunition to his Battery, a very heavy enemy barrage was encountered, during which several pack horses became bogged. Notwithstanding the continued heavy shell fire and that two of his comrades were blown to pieces, Driver Robertson worked on until he had got the horses out and finally delivered the ammunition to the guns. He showed a fine spirit and example of devotion to duty.

Robertson was selected to play for the AIF First XV and played in two of the five King's Cup matches against Canada and New Zealand.

Leslie Seaborn

Leslie Watson Saunderson Seaborn was born in 1877 in Young, New South Wales, to Reverend Frederick Ransom and Eliza Seaborn.

Married and working as a solicitor, Seaborn enlisted in the AIF on 25 May 1917 at age 40 as a Second Lieutenant (Honorary Lieutenant) and was allocated to the 19th Battalion embarking on 16 July 1917.

Seaborn was recommended for the Military Cross on 7 September 1918 which was subsequently awarded on 1 February 1919. The citation read:

> During the attack on Mont St Quentin, near Peronne, on 31 August 1918, this officer showed splendid courage and bravery in holding his position. On reaching the objective, he suddenly found his position surrounded by the enemy. In a few minutes nearly all his men became casualties and with only 6 men and a Lewis gun left, he pluckily attacked the enemy. With sheer gallantry and determination he drove the enemy off inflicting heavy casualties on them with Lewis gun fire, and cleared the situation. Having strongly organised his position, he then assisted a stretcher bearer to get the wounded away, carrying to the support line, over exposed ground, and under heavy enemy machine gun and rifle fire. His splendid courage inspired the men with the greatest confidence.

Seaborn managed the AIF Reserve Team.

Seaborn died on 12 May 1931.

Godfrey 'Babe' See

Godfrey Edward See was born in Armidale, New South Wales, to Mrs C. See.

Working as a brick maker, See enlisted in the AIF as a private on 1 February 1916 and allocated to the 33rd Battalion. He embarked on 4 May 1916 and served in D Company. At some stage he was promoted to Corporal.

On 13 August 1918, Corporal See was recommended for the Military Medal which was subsequently awarded on 23 May 1919. The recommendation read:

> For conspicuous gallantry and devotion to duty during operations against enemy positions south of the Somme east of Hamel on 8 August 1918. Corporal See, with his section, stormed a strong point in Accroche Wood and succeeded in killing four and capturing 16 of the enemy. He led his section close to the barrage and on reaching Rat Wood cooperated in the capture of a battery of 4.2's which had been firing point blank killing a gunner and capturing 7 others. With his section he captured altogether 27 prisoners. Throughout Corporal See displayed courage, energy, determination and leadership, and greatly inspired his men.

See was promoted to Sergeant sometime between August 1918 and January 1919.

See was selected to play for the AIF Trench Team in the match against the French Army on 19 January 1919. See was also selected for the AIF First XV and played in all five of the King's Cup matches. On the AIF Team's Australia Tour See played in six of the eight matches.

See played one match for New South Wales in 1919.

Thomas 'Tom' Stenning

Thomas Stenning was married and working as a plasterer when he enlisted in the AIF as a private on 20 September 1915 and was allocated to the 31st Battalion. He embarked on 14 March 1916.

Stenning was selected for the AIF First XV and played in two of the five King's Cup matches. On the AIF Team's Australia Tour Stenning played in all eight matches

Dudley 'Dud' Suttor

Dudley Colin Suttor was born on 10 April 1892 to Walter Sydney Suttor and Louisa Ellen Suttor nee Monro in Cowra, NSW. He was educated at the Sydney Church of England Grammar School (Shore), Sydney.

Suttor became a fruit grower near Bathurst, NSW, and played rugby for Bathurst. He represented NSW in 1912 playing eight matches on the wing. A journalist recorded that,

> Suttor, the left wing three quarter back, was the crackerjack player of the side. He scored three brilliant tries and would have scored three dozen had J. Flynn never been born. Suttor as a winger is the ideal, a man who shoots off the mark like lead out of a Winchester, fast as a Zebra, and generally, a reckless, daring smashing player.

Suttor had that great attribute that all top-class wingers need—speed—and he could use his extreme pace to fashion scoring chances where none seemed to exist. A contemporary of fly half Bill Tasker, Suttor made his New South Wales debut in the same match but missed selection for the 1912 Australian team that toured America. Bathurst was apparently so upset over his omission that the city immediately swung over to rugby league. Perhaps that was no bad thing, as the tour was little short of a debacle, and by the time 1913 rolled around Suttor was both fresh and hungry for success.

Although he continued to play in the country, Suttor's abilities were well known in town. When South Sydney wing R.D. Fusedale did not have a particularly good match in the first contest against the visiting New Zealand Maori team, Suttor was called up. Suttor's first real chance came from a slick move worked by Fred Wood and Tasker, which gave the speedy Bathurst man a modicum of space. It was all he needed, as he burst clear of the defence and scored after a 50-yard run that had the crowd on its feet. In the second spell, he again made a classy finishing run after good work by the inside backs who had created space. His defence also won acclaim on many occasions. Praised on all sides as the star turn of a hard-fought match, Suttor was always going to be chosen for the 1913 New Zealand tour.

Suttor toured New Zealand as a wing three quarter with the 1913 Waratahs and earned his international cap (Wallaby number 129). He played all the main matches and, with Ernie Carr playing every match, Queensland winger Lou Meibusch did not get a look in. Suttor did little early on, as most of the play tended to run Carr's way, but he made a mark in the second Test. Finally given a chance to show off his great pace, Suttor scored one of Australia's three tries that day after receiving the ball from his centres and being given half a yard to move in. Once again, that was all he needed as he raced off to score. He scored again after coming on as a replacement at Timaru—the injury finishing any hopes Meibusch may have entertained of winning a Test spot—and Suttor had a stand-out game at Christchurch. He scored two fine tries, once after getting an overlap and the other after receiving a cut-out pass from Larry Wogan, and both times he was too quick for the chasers or the cover.

Australia claimed an historic 16-5 win, its first over the All Blacks in New Zealand, and was value for every point. The tour finished with a match against a moderate Marlborough side at Blenheim, where Suttor and Carr enjoyed both the firm ground and the space created by the centres to register hat-tricks. Naturally the two wingers were the day's star players and Suttor was the leading try scorer on the tour with seven tries.

Whatever his reputation after the New Zealand tour, Suttor had a less impressive home season in 1914. He was a member of the New South Wales side that faced the All Blacks in the tour opener and then played for Central-Western in the second tour match. This was a disaster as far as Suttor was concerned; he spent most of the afternoon trying to combat two or three attackers and the home side, completely outclassed, lost by 10-59. The All Blacks scored 15 tries and Suttor's marker, Henry Taylor, scored five times. Even though his defence had been a feature in New Zealand, Suttor was condemned on this showing and Queensland fullback Eric Francis was promoted to the Test wing spot. Suttor was also left out of the New South Wales side for the return match, although he did keep his place for the Queensland game.

Enlisting in the AIF on 16 June 1915, Suttor served as a driver with the 15th Australian Army Service Corps train, which was attached to the 5th Infantry Brigade, 2nd Division. He embarked on 30 September 1915 and his unit was involved in the defence of the Suez Canal before deploying to the Western Front where it took part in the battles of Pozières, Bullecourt, Menin Road and Amiens. Between October 1916 and January 1917 he is recorded as being admitted into hospital with mild 'VDH'—Valvular Disease of the Heart.

In 1919, Suttor was selected for the AIF Trenches Team and played against the French Army on 19 January 1919. Suttor was also selected for the AIF First XV team and played in all five of the King's Cup matches.

Suttor played the first two matches during the AIF Team's Australia Tour. One Australian journalist wrote: 'The final between the Diggers and Our Boys resulted in a ding dong struggle during the first half, but in the second spell the fighting boys, with a brisk breeze behind them, charged the line repeatedly, and had all the best of the game. Suttor electrified the shivering barrackers with his dashing sprints goal-wards.'

Suttor withdrew from the AIF Team's Australia tour after the second match in May 1919 and returned to his orchards in Bathurst.

Little is known about Suttor after the war other than he married Elizabeth Palmer in 1921 at the All Saints' Cathedral in Bathurst, NSW, and they later divorced.

Ever the sportsman, and excellent swimmer and body surfer, Suttor passed away on 15 April 1962 just after his 70th birthday whilst competing in a 55 yard RSL swimming race at the Dee Why pool.

John 'Bluey' Thompson

John Thompson was born on 16 June 1886 at Warwick, Queensland. Thompson began his rugby career with the Toowoomba Rugby Football Cub as a short, chunky prop forward with pace and a thick mop of red hair that inevitably saw him dubbed 'Bluey'. His good form for Toowoomba in the Country Rugby Carnival in 1908 led to his selection in a powerful Queensland Country side that contained a number of outstanding players: 'Mick' Bolewski, 'Ooler' Olsen, Jack Egan, Tom 'Rusty' Richards and 'Brickey' Farmer.

When the country boys trounced Metropolitan Brisbane 16-3, Thompson and his teammates expected to secure a majority of places in the Queensland team to play New South Wales. Much to their dismay, only four country players were chosen.

The disappointed country players became easy prey for scouts from the newly-formed Rugby League in Brisbane. The Queensland Rugby Union selectors chose Thompson in the Queensland 'B' side that met New South Wales in the mid-week match but Thompson quickly joined the Rugby League ranks along with Bolewski and Olsen.

There was no club rugby league in Brisbane in 1908 but Thompson, Olsen and Bolewski were included in the Queensland Rugby League team that played New South Wales in Sydney. Thompson captained Queensland surmounting his age of 19 years.

However, Thompson soon regretted his short foray into the ranks of rugby league and pleaded for re-instatement in the amateur game. Although the QRU refused to re-instate a number of players who regretted the switch to league, Thompson was granted a reprieve on account of his youth.

Resuming his rugby union career, Thompson continued as a prop forward. He made his State debut in 1910 in Queensland's 13-8 loss to the Maoris at the Exhibition Ground as a replacement for Sam Topham. Selected for the southern tour, Thompson played the first of his nine matches against New South Wales at the Sydney University Oval. The home side won 34-14 and Thompson missed selection in the return encounter.

The next two seasons proved lean times for Thompson but, in 1913, he changed to the Brothers Club in Brisbane, along with Toowoomba winger Herb Callaghan, and switched to the side of the scrum as a flanker.

The fiery Thompson, red hair aflame, proved a sensation in his new position as a marauding flanker and, for him, 1914 proved a stellar year in which he represented Queensland in six matches and was chosen for Australia in the first two Tests against the touring All Blacks (Wallaby number 141).

In the first Test in Sydney, Billy Thompson formed the Wallaby backrow along with Harold Baker and number 8, Fred Thompson. The Australian selectors wanted to retain the same team for the second Test only for three New South Wales forwards—Fred Thompson, 'Doss' Wallach and Bill Watson—to announce their unavailability. Three players from the Brothers Club replaced them—Bill Morrissey, Clinker Birt and Sam Kreutzer—bringing the number of Brothers players in the Test side to six. Although Thompson was selected for the third Test, he was unable to come down to Sydney for the match.

After the outbreak of war, Brothers continued with two teams of equal strength in the Brisbane competition in 1915 and Thompson played for Brothers. Although there were no interstate fixtures that year, Thompson was selected in a powerful South Queensland team that toured Central Queensland. He finished the year as a member of the Brothers 'A' team that retained the Hospital Cup with a win over Easts.

Thompson enlisted in 1916, serving with the 15th Field Ambulance. Arriving in France in October 1917, his division would be involved in the Battle of Polygon Wood before moving on to Villers-Bretonneux and then to Amiens. Thompson was promoted to Lance Corporal in January 1918.

Thompson was selected to play for the AIF Trench Team in the match against the French Army on 19 January 1919. Thompson was also selected for the AIF First XV and played in three of the five King's Cup matches. On the AIF Team's Australia Tour Thompson played in seven of the eight matches.

After a very long life, Thompson died in 1978 aged 92.

'Jack' Watkins

Watkins was selected to play for the AIF First XV and played in three of the five King's Cup matches.

William 'Billy' Watson

William Thornton Watson was born on 10 November 1887 at Nelson, New Zealand, son of Tasmanian-born Robert Watson, blacksmith, and his Victorian wife Annie, née Harford.

At age 24, he relocated to Sydney and joined the inner-city Newtown Rugby Union Club, playing at prop. In 1912, he made his representative debut for New South Wales and that same year was selected for the 1912 Australia rugby union tour of Canada and the USA (Wallaby number 123). The American newspapers, aware of Australia's Olympic gold medal for rugby, dubbed the visitors 'the world champions of rugby' but the tour was a disappointment with the squad billeted out in college fraternity houses where the hospitality played havoc with team discipline. As a result, the team lost against two California University sides and three Canadian provincial sides but rose to the occasion for the sole Test of the tour—the November 1912 clash against the United States at Berkeley, won 12-8. Watson played in the sole Test match of the tour as well as ten other matches of the total sixteen.

Watson made appearances for New South Wales in 1913 against the visiting New Zealand Maori side. He toured New Zealand with the 1913 Wallabies captained by Larry Dwyer, appearing in a total of eight of the nine matches played. This included all three Tests where he packed the scrum in a consistent front-row combination with Harold George and David Williams.

When the All Blacks toured to Sydney in 1914, Watson was picked to play against them for New South Wales, as a Wallaby in the first Test at the Sydney Cricket Ground, and in a Metropolitan Sydney side in a mid-week game. The outbreak of the First World War on 4 August 1914 forced the All Black tour to be cut short.

Three days after war was declared, Watson enlisted in the Australian Naval and Military Expeditionary Force (AN&MEF). The AN&MEF's objectives being the capture of the radio stations in German New Guinea. Watson saw action seizing the German wireless stations in New Britain and New Ireland.

With the AN&MEF's objectives quickly achieved the organisation was disbanded and Watson was discharged in January 1915. Watson then enlisted in the Australian Imperial Force (AIF) as a gunner and reinforcement for the 1st Divisional Artillery. He embarked from Sydney on 26 June 1915, landed at Gallipoli on 14 August 1915, and two days later joined the 1st Field Artillery Brigade. He was involved in the defence of ANZAC Cove and the battle of Sari Bair.

After service at Gallipoli in March 1916 he proceeded with his unit to France where his temporary promotion to sergeant was confirmed on 22 April 1916. During operations at the Somme from 26 October 1916 to 15 January 1917, Watson was awarded the Distinguished Conduct Medal for his actions. The citation reads:

> For conspicuous gallantry and devotion to duty. He displayed great gallantry and coolness in going to the assistance of wounded men, under heavy fire. He has set a splendid example throughout.'

He was then posted to England for officer training and was commissioned as a 2nd Lieutenant on 7 September 1917. He then joined the 2nd Field Artillery Brigade in Belgium where he was wounded in action on 17 November 1917, receiving a severe gunshot wound to his abdomen.

Promoted to Lieutenant on 7 December 1917, he returned to duty in April 1918 and was at Foucaucourt on 27 August 1918, acting as forward observation officer with the infantry. When the advance was impeded by enemy machine-gun fire, Watson worked his way forward and directed three batteries barraging the German machine-gun posts. For his conduct Watson was awarded the Military Cross. The citation reads:

> For conspicuous gallantry and devotion to duty at Foucaucourt on 27 August 1918, when he accompanied the attacking infantry as Forward Observation Officer. The enemy offered strong resistance, frequently holding up the advance with machine-gun fire. In one case he worked his way forward several hundred yards in front of our outposts, directing the fire of three batteries, which gave great assistance to the infantry by barraging machine guns nests and strong posts. He showed fine courage and initiative throughout.

In one of the final actions of the war, Watson would be awarded a Bar to his Military Cross for his actions at Nauroy in France near the St. Quentin Canal and the Hindenburg Line. The citation reads:

> For conspicuous gallantry at Nauroy near Bellicourt, on the night of 2-3 October 1918. His battery was the centre of an enemy bombardment which continued for over four hours. Though badly gassed himself, he tried to save the life of a wounded officer. He showed great energy and devotion to duty and stayed with his battery until the next day, when it was withdrawn from the line.

At war's end and during the long process of returning 250 000 Australian troops from Europe, Watson was selected as captain of the AIF First XV. The team represented the Australian Forces in the King's Cup Rugby Competition among the nations represented in the allied armies with teams representing the British, Canadian, New Zealand and South African forces as well as the Royal Air Force. When playing with the AIF team as a front-row forward, Watson must have suffered excruciating pain as he was covered in festering sores, the after-effects of mustard gas. Major Walter 'Wally' Matthews, the team manager, frequently had to open these festering sores with a sterilised penknife before Watson took to the field. On the AIF Team's Australia Tour Watson played in five of the eight games, all as captain.

After returning to civilian life Watson took up first grade rugby again and at age 32 joined the new venture Glebe-Balmain club—the two prior clubs had merged as a result of the player losses each had suffered in the War. Watson was the captain of Glebe-Balmain from 1919 to 1924. In 1920 he was selected as captain of the New South Wales state team and led them in three matches against a touring All Blacks side. With no Queensland Rugby Union administration or competition in place from 1919 to 1929, the New South Wales Waratahs were the top Australian representative rugby union side of the period. A number of their fixtures of the 1920s played against full international opposition were decreed by the

Australian Rugby Union in 1986 as official Test matches. Though he was not aware of it at the time, Watson's three appearances as captain of New South Wales were Test match captaincy fixtures. All told, Watson played 46 matches for Newtown, 13 for Glebe-Balmain and 22 matches for New South Wales. He played 24 matches for Australia including the three NSW Tests of 1920 plus five other pre-war Tests.

After the war Watson lived in Papua New Guinea working in a range of industries including copra production, cattle ranching and prospecting for gold in the then practically unknown Owen Stanley Ranges. In September 1929 he married American-born Cora May Callear in Sydney. They relocated to Columbiana, Ohio, in 1935.

At the start of the Second World War, Watson returned to Australia and served in the 2nd Australian Garrison Battalion from March 1940. In June 1940, his pre-war New Guinea experience (and his ability to speak local New Guinea dialect) was put to use when he was posted to the Papuan Infantry Battalion (PIB), a force of native soldiers, and Australian officers and NCOs. Watson took command of the unit in 1942.

With Japan's invasion of Papua and New Guinea on 21 July 1942 and the commencement of the Kokoda Track campaign, the PIB were the first Australian Army unit to make contact with the Japanese. The battalion, an element of Maroubra Force, was dispersed between Awala and the north coast when the Japanese landed at Buna and Gona on 22 July 1942. Outnumbered, the PIB fell back before the advancing Japanese; its remnants linked up with leading troops of the 39th Battalion, fought rear-guard actions at Gorari and Oivi, and rejoined Lieutenant Colonel W. T. Owen, the Maroubra Force commander at Deniki.

Having abandoned the position prematurely, Owen reoccupied Kokoda on 28 July 1942, his force having been reduced to about 80 men. The Japanese attacked that evening and when Owen was killed, Watson took command. Watson led a fighting retreat back towards the village of Deniki, a mile or so back along the Kokoda Track towards Isurava. Watson remained in command until 4 August 1942 when he was relieved by the arrival of a more senior commander.

Major W.T. Watson, DSO, MC and Bar, DCM, Commanding Officer 1st Papuan Infantry Battalion, Bisiatabu, New Guinea, 26 October 1943. (AWM 058751)

For his bravery and leadership during the withdrawal, Watson was awarded the Distinguished Service Order. He was promoted to Major on 1 September 1942 and remained as the Commanding Officer of the PIB. The PIB subsequently carried out useful work, patrolling the flanks of the Australian-American forces as they pushed northward against the Japanese.

Watson relinquished his command on 30 March 1944 and on 7 July was transferred to the reserve list. After the war, he returned to the United States and was appointed as Australian Vice-Consul in New York until 1952. Survived by his wife, daughter and son, Watson died on 9 September 1961 in the Veterans Administration Hospital, Brooklyn, New York.

www.ingramcontent.com/pod-product-compliance
Lightning Source LLC
Chambersburg PA
CBHW060802150426
42813CB00059B/2862